In the morass of recently published books on parenting, this exceedingly practical manual emerges as a beacon of guidance, wisdom, and common sense. Parents of all backgrounds will benefit from the time-tested methods presented. I have interacted with children raised in this method firsthand and can attest to scores of well-adjusted children who are a joy to their parents. I wholeheartedly endorse this manual without reservation.

Jonathan L. Scott, M.D., Ph.D.
Los Angeles, California

Medical school in no way prepared me for one of the more demanding aspects of my practice: dealing with infant feeding. The theory of feeding a baby whenever it cries, which was standard teaching, was not only without justification—it simply did not meet the needs of my patients. Since being introduced to the principles of *On Becoming Babywise*, I have been convinced of its effectiveness in establishing sleep patterns and in decreasing the frequency of problems associated with infant feeding. If thriving children and happy, rested parents were not enough, my greatest commendation of *On Becoming Babywise* is that my own children are being raised by these precepts.

Craig Lloyd, M.D.
Brisbane, Australia

As a pediatrician, I cannot argue with the success of *On Becoming Babywise*. It is such a practical approach to parenting. It provides infants with needed structure and stability and brings the joy and love so needed in our homes today. The effects of not using *On Becoming Babywise* show up very quickly. That is why I have made these principles a priority of discussion in every well-child care visit. Parents constantly tell me, "It changed our lives."

Janet Dunn, M.D.
Chatsworth, California

As an obstetrician and a mother, my concern for a healthy outcome continues beyond the moment of delivery. Because the principles of *On Becoming Babywise* are so effective, I consider it part of my extended health care for the entire family. The principles are simple—yet amazing. They consistently produce babies who are healthy, content, and who sleep through the night at an early age. Feeding a baby on demand simply cannot compare to the overall healthy benefits of *Babywise*. The concepts take the guesswork out of early parenting and provide new moms the confidence of knowing what happens next. Not following the principles of *Babywise* is a potential health concern.

Sharon Nelson, M.D.
Glendale, California

As a nurse-midwife, childbirth educator, and mom, I encourage my patients in the direction of *On Becoming Babywise*. Why would any parent not want a happy, healthy, and content baby who sleeps through the night in eight weeks? Why would any parent not desire the confidence *Babywise* offers? *Babywise* provides wisdom, common sense, confidence—all refreshing and hopeful words for expectant parents to feast upon.

Diane Dirks, R.N., C.N.M.
Pasadena, California

I am a practicing pediatrician and assistant professor of pediatrics. Residents and new mothers I work with have found *On Becoming Babywise* overwhelmingly successful. My residents report a positive difference in the confidence of new mothers who work with this plan compared to those who do not. The freedom *Babywise* provides a new mother is so refreshing. Life is predictable, allowing her to be proactive in parenting, not reactive, which usually produces less than desirable results. My parents become baby wise with *Babywise*.

Linda Meloy, M.D.
Richmond, Virginia

As a mother, I have parented both ways. As a certified lactation educator, I only recommend *On Becoming Babywise*. I know how discouraging it is to feed a baby around the clock with no apparent advantage. I know how tired a young mom can get and how that affects her milk supply. I also know how discouraging the first eighteen months of parenting can be without a plan. I know because with my first child I did everything the opposite of *Babywise*. Before my second baby was born, I was introduced to the concepts presented in this book. Applying the principles revolutionized my thinking. Instead of being in baby bondage, I was liberated to be the mother God wanted me to be. I have consistently used *Babywise* with the women I counsel. These mothers have met with tremendous success, whether bottle- or breast-feeding. *Babywise* is proactive, preventative parenting, minimizing the common problems often associated with breast-feeding.

Barbara Phillips, R.N., C.L.E.
Los Angeles, California

As a practicing pediatrician, husband, and father, I enthusiastically recommend *On Becoming Babywise*. I found the principles contained within to be a sigh of welcome relief to sleepless, weary parents, and more than an ounce of prevention for those who adopt these concepts from the start. I am convinced that the well-tested principles of *Babywise* produce confident parents, secure and content infants, and peaceful and orderly homes.

David Blank, M.D.
Longmont, Colorado

As family physicians and a husband-wife team, we are often asked questions related to parenting and the general care of children. Most of our basic responses are found in *On Becoming Babywise*. For answering parenting questions, it has become a practical guide giving us a sense of competence and confidence as physicians and as parents. When the principles are put into practice, parents reap abundant rewards.

Tony Burden, M.D., and Margaret Burden, M.D.
Bellingham, Washington

My sister-in-law gave me *On Becoming Babywise* when my baby was three months old. I had read lots and lots of books and magazines, talked to many experienced mothers, and asked the help of my pediatrician, but nothing had answered all of my questions—until I read your book. I highly recommend this book to all mothers and mothers-to-be.

A mother from West Covina, California

My husband and I had heard all sorts of horror stories and felt so discouraged and defeated before our baby came. Feeding around the clock, unexplained fussiness, and bondage (to our baby) were not what we wanted. We were sure there had to be a more sane way to parent than that. We were introduced to your concepts a week after our son was born. How timely! As predicted, our baby was sleeping through the night at five weeks. We have order in our family and are not ashamed of it. Thank you for giving us the confidence to do what is best for our son.

A mother from Denver, Colorado

Without reservation I would recommend this program to anyone—because it works. I demand-fed my first three children, not knowing there was another way. I didn't get a complete night's sleep in five years. When friends began to share your principles, I refused to listen to what I thought was simplistic nonsense. I hold a master's degree in early childhood education and your concepts challenged everything I had been taught.

When our friends' first child slept through the night at six weeks, I was enraged. My husband and I watched as their second and third followed the same pattern. They had everything under control, and so few of the problems that we experienced. When I discovered that I was expecting baby number four, I was depressed for months. The only thing I could focus on was the misery of more sleepless nights and demanding children.

I am ashamed to say that it was out of desperation that we applied your parent-directed feeding. I was humbled. Our baby slept through the night at four weeks. We couldn't believe it was that easy. He was a delight, happy and content, something never experienced with the first three. Since then, a fifth child has arrived and, again, success. *On Becoming Babywise* has saved our marriage and family. Thank you.

A mother from Philadelphia, Pennsylvania

My husband and I want to thank you for getting us on the right track from the beginning. It wasn't easy, because all our friends followed the demand-feeding philosophy and said a schedule was bad for the baby. For these families, children were a major interruption. That didn't make sense to us. We stayed with your program and our baby slept eight hours through the night at six weeks, and eleven hours at twelve weeks—just like your book says. My friends said exactly what you predicted: that we were lucky and had an easy baby. But we know otherwise. Thank you for being a source of encouragement.

A mother from Fort Worth, Texas

I was at church holding a crying baby and everyone asked what was wrong with my son. They said they had never before heard him cry. Then they realized it wasn't my son I was holding. Thank you for *On Becoming Babywise.* My wife and I have a happy, contented baby.

Before our son was born we'd heard so many sad stories. My sister had not gone out with her husband alone for three years after the birth of their first son. She went to a mothers' support group but only found other mothers to cry with. No thank you. Not for my wife. We follow the principles of PDF. Because our lives are so predictable and our son responds so well to routine, we had our first date night after three weeks and once a week ever since. Thank you for helping to keep our family a family.

A father from Tacoma, Washington

Our daughter will be one year old at the end of this month and I must tell you that I truly and profoundly enjoyed this year of her life. A big part of the reason is because we followed the principles of *On Becoming Babywise.* It was not only helpful with my daughter, but also helped me understand my frustrations with my firstborn! I kept wondering why he was so demanding. Why would he never sleep at night or take decent naps?

I had nursed my son as often as he needed (so I thought)—anytime and anywhere, day and night—until he was twenty-two months old.

And I gave him attention, both quality and quantity. He slept with us at night but after a few weeks the baby slept with only me at night; my husband was on the couch. I stayed home, gave him a good learning environment, and cooked all natural foods. I did everything the "experts" said to do. But they were so wrong. In the end, it was all for nothing. The only thing I succeeded in doing was to raise a demanding, out-of-control toddler who is not pleasant to be with.

I don't share this to burden you, but to encourage you. Please get the *Babywise* principles out to young families of our nation (Canada) and yours, so they will not have to suffer what we did. Thank you for your sensible teaching.

A mother from Vancouver, British Columbia

My husband and I want to thank you for helping us gain the confidence to parent. Your book has been around to all the expectant moms at our preschool. Everyone wants to know why our son, Jonathan, is such a good baby. My husband and I have found parenting to be a joyful experience. It makes so much sense to work from a plan and provide order for our child. Because of that, I have more energy for my husband, my friends, and to do the extra things with my son. Thank you.

A mother from Los Angeles, California

My wife and I were introduced to your program while in marriage counseling. It was then that we discovered the trap of child-centered parenting. In the name of "good parenthood," we gave up our marriage—figuratively and nearly literally. We did this for the "baby's good." That sounded sacrificial and was something I wanted to do as a father. But I never realized how faulty that thinking was until I read your first two chapters. Your book makes sense out of nonsense.

After eighteen months of misery, we started our son on a routine. After three nights he began sleeping through the night and my wife began to sleep with me—but this time alone. What a difference a good night's sleep makes to a toddler's disposition! We had a new son. Get these vital principles out to every family of childbearing age.

A father from Atlanta, Georgia

I am a grandmother with fourteen grandchildren. I must admit, the evidence of your principles is apparent in our family. My second daughter was introduced to your material in Florida and brought it back to the rest of the family. I was surprised that your teaching is needed. You tell parents to do what we did years ago when there were no books or tapes, just practical wisdom. Thank you for your practical advice. You have helped make grandparenting a joy.

A grandmother from Raleigh, North Carolina

Thank you so much for your book. What an eye opener! With the utmost love and the best intentions, I had gone wrong in most ways with regard to feeding/sleeping patterns and breast-feeding. I followed the demand-feeding methodology. How deceived I was. Your book arrived at a point of desperation, with our baby waking eight to twelve times nightly and a four-year-old coming into our bed each night. Existing on almost no sleep, our marriage was suffering and we both decided we couldn't live this way anymore. A counselor pointed us to *On Becoming Babywise.* It turned our lives around. Please use this letter to encourage young couples to grasp and hold on to the principles of *Babywise.*

A mother from Christ Church, New Zealand

ON BECOMING

BABY WISE

BOOK ONE

LEARN HOW OVER 500,000
*babies were trained to sleep through
the night the natural way*

■

GARY EZZO AND
ROBERT BUCKNAM, M. D.

Multnomah Publishers *Sisters, Oregon*

To:

Dr. Fred and Mary Barshaw—
for their many years
of lighting the way.

ON BECOMING BABYWISE

published by Multnomah Publishers, Inc.

© 1995, 1998 by Gary Ezzo and Robert Bucknam, M.D.

International Standard Book Number: 1-57673-458-7

Cover photo by David Hanover, Tony Stone Images

Multnomah is a trademark of Multnomah Publishers, Inc., and is registered in
the U.S. Patent and Trademark Office. The colophon is a trademark of
Multnomah Publishers, Inc.

Printed in the United States of America

For information:
MULTNOMAH PUBLISHERS, INC.
POST OFFICE BOX 1720
SISTERS, OREGON 97759

98 99 00 01 02 03 04 05 — 12 11 10

ACKNOWLEDGMENTS

The only justification for revising a book is to improve it. It is our hope that the changes made within have accomplished that aim. This second edition reflects impressive advances that have been made since the first edition went to press. Our changes are predominately practical, not philosophical. Structurally, we combined chapters 3 and 4, expanded the section on monitoring your baby's healthy growth in chapter 5, and expanded the problem-solving questions found in chapter 10. We incorporated a number of studies, including the ones we commissioned in our pursuit of establishing *Babywise* norms for sleep, weight gain, and average length of time our mothers breast-fed their babies. Overall, this edition brings the same message, but better said. And we have many people to thank for making it a better tool in the hands of young parents.

We owe a special debt of gratitude to Dr. Eleanor Womack, a mother of triplets, twins, and two singletons. Due to her firsthand experience and expertise, we asked Dr. Womack if she would write a chapter for us dealing with multiple births. She consented, and we are very grateful for her help in this area. (See chapter 9, "Multiple Birth: The Endless Party.") We also wish to thank Anne Marie Ezzo for her contribution to this book. In addition, we wish to thank Barbara Phillips and Beth Branch for their contributions. A special thanks to Diane Wiggins, our wonderful editor. Finally, it is with great appreciation that we acknowledge and thank the medical advisory board, including: Kenneth Beckett, M.D.; David Blank, M.D.; Tony Burden, M.D.; Margaret Burden, M.D.; Kathryn Cashner, M.D.; Donald Cline, M.D.; John Curlin, M.D.; Craig Cook, M.D.; Ron Fessenden, M.D.; Donald Frame, M.D.; Carl Hays, M.D.;

Earl Hoffer, M.D.; Bruce Jung, M.D.; Peter Kim, M.D.; Paula Kruppstadt, M.D.; Pennock Laird, M.D.; Saphry May Liauw, M.D.; Brad Lowery, M.D.; Mike McCoy, M.D.; Linda Meloy, M.D.; Jim Pearson, M.D.; Carl Pfansteil, M.D.; Bonnie Premo, M.D.; Tom Reed, M.D.; Van Schalin, M.D.; John Scott, M.D.; Chris Smith, M.D.; Rusty Turner, M.D.; Jeff Welsh, M.D.; Robin Welsh, M.D.; Ginger Williams, M.D.; and Eleanor Womack, M.D. In addition, we wish to thank Carol Clark and Carol Parkinson for their wonderful insights and contributions.

CONTENTS

Foreword

After completing medical school and serving my residency in obstetrics and gynecology, I felt knowledgeable enough to be a parent. Between my wife's degree in child development and my medical training, how hard could this parenting thing be? We would just do what comes naturally and follow our instincts. Right? Wrong!

Soon after the birth of our first son, we quickly found our enthusiasm and confidence turned into exhaustion and frustration. Mom was up three times at night and the baby was cranky during the day. The unsolicited advice typically offered was to feed the baby more often since he was obviously hungry. We did feed him, around the clock, every two hours. As we found out later, that was the cause of the problem, not the cure.

Scientists can put a man on the moon, but they cannot answer the most basic problems of early parenting: how to have a happy and contented baby who sleeps continually through the night like the rest of the family and a mother who is not in a perpetual state of exhaustion.

Through our common interest in children and parenting, my wife and I became acquainted with the work and accomplishments of Gary and Anne Marie Ezzo of Growing Families International. The Ezzos' basic and loving concepts for nurturing newborns virtually eliminated the problems listed above and many more. I have personally observed infants who were guided by the Ezzos' principles and those who were not. It became obvious that parents equipped with the right information do make a difference.

I have since made the transition from obstetrics to pediatrics and with the switch came the medically sound principles of *Babywise*. They work consistently, not only for the thousands of children already touched by Growing Families International, but also for my four children, my colleagues' children, my friends' children, and now, for all my patients.

To say the least, *Babywise* has brought a needed reformation to pediatric counsel given to new parents. When parents come in looking exhausted and discouraged and tell me their woeful stories of sleepless nights and fussy babies, I can give them a positive prescription that cures the problem—I hand them *On Becoming Babywise*.

Robert Bucknam, M.D.
Louisville, Colorado

Preface

Yes, one day people will stop you on the street, at the grocery store, and in the church nursery to comment, "Your baby is so content." Then they will insult you with the following statement: "You're so lucky to have such an easy baby. What? Sleeping through the night already? How old is he? You're really lucky!"

As philosopher Immanuel Kant pointed out, the actual proves the possible. With *On Becoming Babywise,* we no longer count the success stories in thousands, but in tens of thousands. *On Becoming Babywise* is not a book of luck but of principle. Luck has nothing to do with the benefits described above—right parenting does. What you do in the first days, weeks, and months of your baby's life will impact the rest of your parenting years.

This is more than a sleep-training book. Getting your baby to sleep through the night within seven to nine weeks is the easiest part of parenting. Realizing the awesome duty of raising a responsible human being is more difficult.

This book will not provide you with a list of rules. We wish parenting were that easy. Our purpose is to get you started on the right track, beginning with the preparation of your mind, which is far more important than the preparation of the nursery. Your baby will not care if his head rests on designer sheets or on Disney characters. His behavior will not be ordered by his wardrobe or by his bedroom accessories, but by the mind-set that dictates how you live your life.

Our personal perspective of life in general governs how we relate to our children, to our spouse, and to others. This book assumes that the reader is family-centered and is not child-centered or mother-centered. That means you regard your baby as a welcome member of the family and not the center of the family universe. That perspective is foundational to the concepts presented in this book.

In discussing infant and maternal physiology, we will demonstrate how order and stability are mutual allies of every newborn's metabolism. In particular, we will note how an infant's body responds to the influences of parental routine or the lack thereof.

In the latter chapters, we will explore the everyday aspects of infant management. Included is an explanation of the three basic elements of daytime activities for newborns: feeding time, waketime, and naptime.

The questions at the end of each chapter emphasize the key themes found in your reading. We encourage you to take the time to go through and write out the answers. You will feel more confident when you know what to do and why you should do it. We designed the study questions to serve as an aid in gaining that confidence.

On Becoming Babywise is more than an infant-management concept; it is a mind-set for responsible parenthood. The principles presented will help any parent develop a plan that meets both the needs of a new baby and of the entire family. This plan will not leave mom ragged at the end of the day nor in bondage to her child. Nor will dad be excluded from his duties. These principles have worked for thousands of parents and, when faithfully applied, will also work wonderfully for you!

Gary Ezzo

Introducing Chelsea and Marisa

Two fictional characters will appear throughout this book. They are Chelsea and Marisa, cousins born within a week of each other. Chelsea's parents followed the principles we will outline. Marisa's parents did not. Although fictional, the differences stated in the development of these characters are reflective of several hundred testimonies we have received from parents.

Chapter One

Your Baby Needs a Family

With a baby in your future, everyone seems to state the obvious: "Life as you know it will never be the same." Of course, the ominous inference of this refrain is that change is not always so good. But shouldn't family life be your joy—abounding in sweet memories and untainted by fear or regret? Why wouldn't you expect bliss from your sweet little blessing?

Being professionals who provide health and educational services to families, we have counseled many parents who started with high hopes and the best intentions to love and nurture their children, only to see their dreams of a beautiful family reduced to a nightmare of survival. Who are these people? They are people like you. The family next door. That neighbor down the street with the wooden stork on her lawn announcing the birth of Alexis. That sweet couple you met in your birthing class. You think they are too sweet. Too kind. They all have the best of intentions. If wishes and dreams were bright lights and lollipops, every day would be bliss. But there's much more to good parenting than just high hopes.

Although the primary emphasis of this book is the nurturance of a newborn, we would be remiss in our educational efforts if we skipped the foundations of what makes hope reality. We are committed to the belief that if you really love your child, you will give him the gift of love, security, and a sense of belonging—give him the assurance that as a husband and wife, you really love each other. The husband-wife union is not just a good first step towards child-rearing. It is a necessary one.

Too often, parents lose sight of this fact, getting lost in a parenting wonderland of photos, footsteps, and first words. Baby becomes central to their existence. Yet the greatest overall influence you will have on your children will not come in your role as an individual parent, but in your joint role as husband and wife. The husband-wife team is the model upon which much of this material is based. However, if you happen to be a single parent or your spouse is absent from the home, don't assume this book isn't for you. Your job as parent may be more challenging, but the principles presented in this and subsequent chapters are universally true and can be applied in all families.

Marriage represents a special bond between two people that is matched by no other relationship. At least that was the original idea. Marriage is unique—totally without parallel. It transcends all other relationships. How truly amazing it is! Here's an important outcome of making the most of marriage. *Great marriages produce great parents.*

A healthy husband-wife relationship is essential to the emotional health of children in the home. When there is harmony in the marriage, there is an infused stability within the family. A strong marriage provides a haven of security for children as they grow in the nurturing process. Healthy, loving marriages create a sense of certainty for children. When a child observes the special friendship and emotional togetherness of his parents, he or she is more secure simply because it isn't necessary to question the legitimacy of their parent's commitment to one another.

Why is this important? All children, it seems, are born with a radar device that homes in on parental conflict. If a child perceives more weakness than strength in this relationship, we believe this perception produces a low-level anxiety in the child. Ultimately, the anxiety affects all of the child's learning disciplines. If something happens to mom and dad, every child intuitively knows that his or her whole world will collapse. With this critical relationship constantly in question, the child lives perpetually on the brink of disaster.

You may think: "But we do not argue or slack in our love for each other." Be warned, insecurity is fostered by what is not taking place between couples as much as what is taking place. The goal of parenting is not simply to avoid excessive anxiety, but to create a world of confidence by what we do with each other as much as by what we avoid doing.

Where the marriage is intact, keeping this relationship a priority is your starting point for successful parenting. It almost sounds too easy. To be a good mom or dad, all you need is to continue as before. That's it. But don't kid yourself, this is easier said than done. To improve the quality of the parent-child relationship, parents first must continue to evaluate the quality of their relationship with each other. Would it stand alone without baby? Weak marriages do not build strong families nor do they infuse security into the hearts of children.

Chelsea, one of our fictional characters, has a mom and dad who are committed to each other. From that commitment flows security.

Of all Chelsea's emotional needs, her most basic is knowing mom and dad love each other. Every day, Chelsea observes her mom and dad relating to one another. Confirmation of their love relationship is witnessed daily in the way they talk together, spend time together, and touch. To Chelsea, their commitment to one another is clear. It is not an unanswered question in her tiny heart.

While Chelsea's mom may indeed spend many hours each day loving and nurturing her; all that time and attention, though beautiful, can not by itself meet Chelsea's basic emotional needs. Likewise, her dad can buy dolls, bikes, and books, then play all day at Chelsea's side, but he still will not provide her heart's fulfillment. For Chelsea to be satisfied beyond her own understanding, she needs simply to watch her parents enjoying each other's company. Simple. Sweet. Everyone wins.

Our belief then, is basic. When the marriage relationship is beautiful what impressionable child would not desire to share in its joy? When two are beautifully one, what child would not seek the comforts of this togetherness? The best years of parenting flow out of the best years of marriage. Protect it!

Child-Centered Parenting

Too often when a child enters a family, parents leave their first love: each other. The spotlight shifts to illuminate the children, and the marriage gets lost in space. Typically—and ironically—this occurs in the name of good parenting. In reality, this shift offers devastating results. From its start, the family is breaking apart. This type of parenting puts all other family relationships at risk. Rather than welcoming children to the family, children are treated as the center of the family universe. This is the heart of child-centered parenting.

With child-centered or mother-centered parenting, parents intensely pursue the child's happiness, taking great pains to avoid stress or emotional discomfort in the child's life. Certainly, who doesn't want a happy child whose life is stress free? Would anyone argue against this desire? We would hope not. The issue, then, is not the loftiness of the goal, for that is what this book is pursuing. Our caution centers on the methods used to reach that goal. In this arena there are many opinions.

Marisa's parents have adopted the child-centered approach. As a result, Marisa will never have to wait for anything. If she wants something, it is given to her on demand. Baby-sitters? They make Marisa uneasy. So an evening out alone together simply is not an option. Either her parents will take her everywhere they go, or they will miss a function due to Marisa's inability to take part. As for eating, if Marisa suddenly rejects her bananas, she'll be offered a variety of options until her particular preference is revealed. Then mom will stock the shelves full of Marisa's delight, only to learn days later that the child's pleasure is back to bananas. Welcome to the circus.

Sadly, Marisa's parents are not aware of the disabling impact their attitude has on their daughter. Instead of building Marisa into a self-assured adult, they are fostering the emotionally crippling attitude of *me-ism*. Every day, Marisa's understanding of her place in life is shaped by the feedback she gets from those around her. If she believes she is central to the family universe, her self-centered feeling will carry over into every relationship in her ever-expanding world.

This is devastating both to the family and to Marisa. Other people simply will not matter to Marisa. When siblings and peers come along, look out. Their very presence will challenge Marisa's stronghold on the family nucleus. There is only one center, and she is it. In the big world, Marisa will also struggle, ill-prepared for the give-and-take necessary in any healthy, enduring relationship. No one will cater to her as instantly as mom and dad. Given her demeanor, no one may care to help her at all. This leaves Marisa with an endless string of frustrating circumstances shaping her life.

Across town, Chelsea's mom and dad are working to integrate Chelsea into the existing family structure. She is a welcome member of the family, learning from the start that giving is equally as important as receiving. What a joy she is to have around. Everyone comments on her peace and joy. And why not? Chelsea understands she is a member of the family team. She already has a sense of belonging and purpose for her life. This *we-ism* approach teaches Chelsea to foster close and loving relationships which endure the test of time.

Friendship and Conformity

Every responsible human being has acquired certain virtues useful in getting along well with others. Topping the list are kindness, goodness, gentleness, charity, honesty, honor, and respect for others. All are reasonable and desirable tools for successful living. However, acquisition of these traits is not a goal best left to chance. Parents must train these attributes into the heart of their child.

Chelsea's parents understand that virtues must be nurtured into her tiny heart. The virtues are not inherent in her life or any new life. Therefore, Chelsea's parents must govern and monitor her until they are assured she bears the self-control and moral awareness needed to govern herself. Right from the start, freedoms come gradually. From the playpen to the living room floor and then to the backyard, Chelsea's boundaries are expanded as she proves capable of handling them. Responsible behavior and good judgment within a specific boundary earns Chelsea, over time, yet another level of freedom. In this way, Chelsea achieves a sense of affirmation within herself. Meanwhile those around her will find joy in her presence, further enhancing her inner well-being.

Back at Marisa's home, her mom and dad continue to strive for buddy status. They yearn for friendship, elevating Marisa to the level of peer. And what could be more noble than a family made up of friends? The idea is especially appealing to a generation that has pondered the considerable lack of friendship with their own parents. However, reducing the parental role to the child's level or raising the child to the status of peer will not, in the end, produce friendship. True friendship cannot be forced before its time.

Time and experience are prerequisites for building any friendship. Children enter this world with neither. Wisdom, self-control, and the experiences earned over time must be trained into a child by those granted this unique privilege—the parents. Responsible parents are their children's teacher. The parents lead and the children, as students, follow. Of course, fun times are welcome. You need to have fun along the way, but never at the expense of needed leadership.

Chelsea's parents understand this, knowing that friendship with their daughter is a gift that only time can give. In the meantime, they must represent her best interests. They set the pace in Chelsea's life and insist on her compliance. Chelsea, in turn, acquires the sense that she belongs to something bigger than herself. She belongs to a family with predetermined guidelines and firmly established order. This realization for Chelsea gives family relationships meaning and purpose. By the end of Chelsea's teen years, a beautiful friendship with her parents will begin to blossom. Indeed, this should be every parent's goal.

Achieving a Balance

No one plans to be child-centered. Since infants are entirely dependent on parental care, their dependency creates for new parents a heightened gratification. What you need is a strategy for avoiding child-centered pitfalls. With a bit of forethought and effort, you can meet all your baby's needs while still maintaining life beyond baby. Here are a few ideas to assist in achieving this balance:

1. *Life doesn't stop once you have a baby.* It may slow down for a few weeks, but it should not stop entirely. When you become a mother, you do not stop being a daughter, a sister, a friend, or a wife. Those relationships, which were important before the baby, still must be maintained.

2. *Date your spouse.* If you had a weekly date night with your spouse before the baby, get back in the swing of it as soon as possible. A friend or relative is quite capable of meeting your child's needs. The baby will not suffer separation anxiety from one night without mom. If you never have had a date night, start now!

3. *Continue those loving gestures you enjoyed before the baby came along.* If you both enjoyed a special activity together, find a way to fit it in. If you a buy a special something for baby, select a little gift for your mate as well. In all that you do, treasure your spouse.

4. *Invite some friends over for food and fellowship.* Times of hospi-

tality force you to plan your child's day around serving others as you work together to prepare your home for the guests.

5. *At the end of each day, spend fifteen minutes sitting with your spouse discussing the day's events.* This special "couch time," which takes place before children are in bed for the evening, acts as a visual expression of your togetherness. To help keep this time free of interruptions explain to your children: "This is Mommy and Daddy's special time together. Daddy will play with you afterward, but Mommy comes first." Children actually are assured of mom and dad's love relationship through this tangible demonstration. In addition, couch time genuinely assists couples in sharing their needs and concerns with each other.

Summary

To excel in parenting, protect your marriage. Your marital togetherness will be a safeguard against child-centered parenting. In addition, a united front better absorbs the inevitable shocks of life. Also resolve to be your child's parent, not a peer. Potential peers are everywhere. Yet the child has only one mom and dad. Don't let your baby down. Governing that life is in your child's best interest.

Friendship with your child is a positive long-term objective, exercise patience. Today your child needs your guiding hand. Yes, welcome him or her as a wonderful addition to the family, but never place your child at its center. Instead, build that team spirit. When parents plan for family unity, everyone wins. Only then will life as you know it never be the same. Really. It just got richer.

Questions for Review

1. Of all Chelsea's primary emotional needs, which is most basic?

2. What happens when a child perceives weakness in his or her parents' relationship?

3. What is the first step to breaking up a family?

4. What emotional disability does child-centered parenting produce?

5. How long should parents act as governors in the lives of their children?

6. What is the role of friendship in the parenting process?

....

Chapter Two

Feeding Philosophies

*D*emand-feeding. Hyperscheduling. Cry feeding. Breast-feeding and bottle. Feeding baby should be easy. Your baby needs food and you have it. So why all the confusion? One reason might be the overabundance of parenting theories. With so many options it is no wonder parents get confused. For example, during pregnancy you may have been encouraged to *demand-feed* your baby and warned not to follow a schedule, especially if you intend to breast-feed. Maybe you heard about a *demand schedule* or a *self-regulating schedule*.

Perhaps you were told to consider *natural feeding* for the baby or to avoid *hyperscheduling*. Of course, hyperscheduling is rigid, and *rigid feeding* is not as good as *cry feeding*. However, the latter is less desirable than *cue feeding*, which is similar to *responsive feeding*. And last but not least, is *bottle-feeding*. Where in the process might this fit in?

When it comes to feeding baby, it isn't any wonder many moms resort to simply winging it. Who can decipher all the terms and techniques? Certainly, establishing good feeding habits should be the easiest feature of child training. That's because the drive to obtain nourishment is one of the strongest drives in all living beings. However, much more is happening during feeding time than just filling up a little tummy. How you choose to feed your baby will have a profound effect on your child's hunger patterns, sleep patterns, and basic disposition.

Defining the Terms

Prior to this century, common sense, not theoretical concepts, was most critical in raising children. Mothers nursed babies when they were hungry, having pre-established guidelines for babies' hunger patterns. A mother shaped her baby's hunger cycles to match her need to care for the entire family. A mom had no cause for clock-watching to know feeding time was at hand. Her schedule was set by domestic duties which ruled her day. Thus, routine feedings fit into her schedule in a way orchestrated to meet her baby's needs alongside those of her entire family.

As the industrial revolution progressed, new infant-management theories evolved. During this century, two theories have dominated American parenting. In the early years, the first theory was introduced by a group of scientists called *behaviorists*. Their belief was that a child was molded by his or her environment. The infant's developing emotions and feelings went unrecognized, over-ruled by specific and controlled care. Such outward structure, behaviorists believed, produced in the child controlled emotions. This was considered desirable.

Based on this theory, American mothers in the 1920s were introduced to a feeding practice called hyperscheduling or *clock feeding* the baby. A strict four-hour feeding schedule was established. Every good mother followed it to the minute. If baby seemed hungry after three hours, too bad. No feeding would occur until that fourth hour had passed. The clock was the final authority with no regard for the baby's, and certainly not the mother's, needs.[1]

By the mid-1940s, a second theory, an adaptation of Sigmund Freud's child-rearing theories, started to nudge out the rigidity of behaviorism. Freud's twentieth-century followers stressed the instinctive, animal-like qualities of infancy as the starting point for child management. Structure was not as important to those theorists as were the child's developing emotions. With revisions made to Freud's theories, the American parent was pulled to the other extreme. Now, the baby was fed at the first indication of fussiness whether or not the baby was actually hungry. Under this theory, nursing the baby satisfied both nutritional needs as well as presumed psychological needs.

To what type of psychological need were these theorists referring? Psychoanalysts attempted to locate the origin and nature of adult neuroses by discovering, through psychoanalysis, significant traumatic experiences in early childhood. Originally, the quest into the past ended in the preschool years (two or three years of age). When no traumatic experiences were found in the average patient, analysts were forced to either abandon their theory or, by faith, move to the conclusion that the original source of traumatic experience was the birthing process itself, as postulated by Austrian psychoanalyst Otto Rank in 1929. Even Freud greeted such a notion with skepticism.

That belief inspired the *neoprimitivistic* school of child care, supported by Ribble (1944); Aldrich (1945); Trainham, Pilafian, and Kraft (1945); and Frank (1945). The title "neoprimitivistic" is not name-calling, but a specific school of thought. This theory postulates that the separation at birth momentarily interrupts the mother-child *in utero* harmony. Therefore, the goal of early parenting is to reestablish that harmony. How is this supposed to be achieved? Only by the constant day-and-night presence and availability of the mother to the child. New mothers are instructed to do whatever it takes to neutralize the supposed trauma of birth and offset its effect. By 1949, the birth-trauma theory, lacking objective verifiable data, was dismissed. But that was not the end of it. Twenty-five years later, it resurfaced. Bearing slight modification, the birth trauma theory now carries a revised banner—*attachment parenting*.

It is important to note that the attachment parenting theory and the *theories of attachment* are not necessarily the same. The first is a parenting philosophy driven by an interesting but unproven philosophical assumption—birth trauma. The second is a generally accepted truth that infants are born with both the capacity and need for warm, loving, and intimate relationships. When these relationships are secured from loving parents, the foundation for all future emotional bonds is established. *On Becoming Babywise* will help you connect with your baby and meet his attachment needs and more.

As a result of the birth trauma speculation, the American mother in the early 1950s began leaning more towards a nonstructured approach in parenting. During this time, Dr. Benjamin Spock rightly rejected behaviorists' assumptions of absolute structure and veered parents toward a healthy mix of structure with flexibility. This was a radical idea in the 1950s and a much needed redirection for mothering.

By 1970, Spock's views were being replaced by demand-feeding. This practice operated on the assumption that baby clearly knows best. Mothers were advised to abandon any parent-guided routine and let the baby's cry be the exclusive signal for nursing. Today, the term demand-feeding carries a variety of meanings. Mothers who have converted from their own style of demand-feeding to a style consistent with what is suggested in *Babywise* offer these definitions.

For example, Julia, a second-time mom, describes what demand-feeding looked like for her. "I demand-fed my first child every three hours." For Julia, demand-feeding offered predictability. In contrast, Barbara, a fourth-time mom, defined her last experience as having some flexibility within defined limits. "I fed my baby on demand whenever he was hungry," she said, "But never sooner than two hours and never longer than four hours."

Allicin, a third-time mom and former attachment-parenting follower, describes a more fatiguing experience. "I nursed my babies whenever they cried or began to fuss. On average, I was told that mothering attachment required me to nurse every two hours around the clock for the first six weeks," says Allicin. "I was exhausted."[2]

Obviously definitions vary from household to household. For the purpose of this book, Allicin's definition of attachment parenting will be used when referring to demand-feeding rather than the other two moderate forms described by Julia and Barbara. When attachment parenting, abbreviated AP, is noted, we are implying that the baby's cry is the primary signal for nursing. This is regardless of whether that cry is for food or the baby's presumed psychological need. The baby is offered the breast simply and immediately without any regard for the amount of time that has elapsed since the last feeding. The next feeding may be in three hours or in thirty minutes.

By the early 1980s, the neoprimitivistic school of infant care and its attachment theories gained more ground. AP theorists today believe that babies are born with lingering womb attachments and that birth only changes the way the attachment need is met. In order for the baby to get the best start in life, an artificial womb-like environment must be created and maintained after birth.[3]

This theory overlooks one all-important consideration. The baby is not in the womb any more because he has developed beyond the need for a womb environment. If nature has taken the baby beyond the womb, then creating an artificial, second womb hinders this natural process of growth and development. Why would a parent wish to stagnate a natural progression in their child's life?

The updated version of attachment parenting is remarkably similar to the 1940s version. Back then, theorists told mothers to carry their babies whenever possible, sleep with them, breast-feed day and night without routine, and continue breast-feeding well into their second, even third or fourth year of life. The child, not the mother, initiated weaning from the breast. Likewise, toilet training was left to the child's whims or expression of interest. These practices exalted the child as central to the family universe. Parenting was fashioned to avoid conflict, anxiety and discomfort, any of which threatened to create in the child a debilitating psychosis in later years.

Attachment theorists subscribe to the doctrine of felt needs as the cue for care and training. Continuous access to the mothers breast and immediate gratification are primary parts of the attachment process. These theories suggest that the sensitivity that helps a mother do the right thing at the right time develops more quickly (and to a greater degree) through nursing. They claim that this is why you supposedly can never nurse too long or too often. All wants are to be interpreted as needs, and each nursing experience is a deposit of love.

This explains why the devout "attachment" mother will respond to her baby's cry with the breast even if it is the third time in an hour. She is acting on the conviction that her child is signaling her with an unpleasant emotion. If it is not dealt with immediately, attachment may not occur. Justified in her thinking by the statement, "Every cry is to be interpreted as a need for breast food or breast comfort," she moves dutifully toward her child, never realizing that her child's lack of contentment is most likely the result of her parenting style. Like many parenting theories in existence, attachment-parenting ideas quickly lose value when overstated or oversimplified.

Among attachment-parenting theorists, child-centered beliefs have encouraged exaggerated concerns about a child's momentary feelings and emotional well-being. Too often, adult-centered feelings—feelings that do not really exist for the child—are attributed to the child. It is not that parents are wrong to be concerned about such things, but such concerns must be aligned with a child's actual vulnerabilities. If they are not, then protection turns to overprotection which leads to exaggerated parenting strategies to the detriment of the child.

Overprotective strategies easily carry over into the toddler and post-toddler years. Imagine the three-year-old boy who signals for a snack by pulling on his mother's blouse. When his mother offers him the breast, if even for a minute, she is acting on the belief that he still has an attachment need. To tell him no, say the theorists, would be to deny him the love he needs.[4]

Obviously, a developing body of theory is not the same thing as a developing body of facts. Possibly the child does have a need. But is it the result of birth trauma or a philosophy of parenting? Might the methods used to manufacture a secure, attached child actually be producing the symptoms of an emotionally-stressed, high-need, insecure baby? These symptoms may include a combination of excessive fussiness and colic-like symptoms; instability in feeding and sleep cycles; waking for night nursing for up to two years; low tolerance for delayed gratification; underdeveloped self-comforting and coping skills; limited self-play adeptness—and one tired mom.

The weakness of the womb-and-birth-trauma theory is found in its very premise. Does the birthing process really create psychologically fragile children? Do the stability of all future human emotions really hinge on the necessity of recreating a second artificial womb?

More likely, newborns have zero memory of birth, let alone the ability to recall anxiety that is specific to the experience. Memory function and synapse development depend on the brain receiving highly oxygenated blood which comes from breathing. Breathing cannot begin until the lungs inflate, which occurs after, not during birth. In addition, higher brain centers are still developing at the time of birth. Even if there is any minimal memory function, enough sophistication for baby to associate birthing with trauma remains highly unlikely.

Just for argument's sake, assume functioning memory in the pre-birth state is possible. If we attribute wishes, hopes, and fears to the unborn, as adult-centered perceptions often do, we can assume that toward the end of pregnancy the child longs to be born. His or her environment is no longer paradise. The squirming, turning, wrenching, jerking, and kicking in the last month forces the assumption that the child is more eager to be freed from this environment than longing to stay in it. The womb restrains and holds the baby back.

What about these memories of restraint created in the last month? Do they produce a reservoir of anxiety? Could womb confinement be the original source of trauma? You see, once you open the door of speculation regarding memory function in a prebirth state, all kinds of theories are possible.

Advocates of the birth trauma theory base their conclusion on hypotheses not facts. They interpret their varied hypotheses as equivalent to having objective and supportive data. Hopeful speculation abounds, based upon a minute amount of objective and verifiable information. To date, no one has demonstrated a relationship between the birthing experience, the lack of a second womb, and subsequent neurosis.

While behaviorists emphasize outward structure and not the inner person, the neoprimitivistic school emphasizes the inner person at the expense of outward structure. As professionals, we believe both approaches are extreme. We believe they are both wrong and harmful to the healthy development of any baby and soon-to-be toddler.

The Babywise Alternative

Some mothers emotionally thrive on an attachment style of parenting. That is not the case for all women. A more user-friendly, less fatiguing alternative is available called *parent-directed feeding* (PDF). Parent-directed feeding is a twenty-four hour infant-management strategy designed to help moms connect with their babies and their babies connect with them. It is a proactive approach to infant care, meeting the needs of the newborn and those of the rest of the family.

It is our experience that both baby and mom do better when a baby's life is guided by a flexible routine. PDF is the center point between hyperscheduling on one extreme and attachment parenting at the other. It has enough structure to bring security and order to your baby's world, yet enough flexibility to give mom freedom to respond to any need at anytime.

A parent-directed strategy brings out the best in both parent and baby because it is child-oriented, not child-centered or mother-centered. With this common sense approach, a mother cooperates with her baby's needs and her baby, in return, learns to cooperate with mother's guidance. The result is true connectedness. With PDF, a mother feeds her baby when he is hungry but takes advantage of the first few weeks to guide the baby's hunger patterns by a basic routine. Because the baby is regarded as a welcome member of the family, but not the center of it; and because he is not as emotionally fragile as attachment theorists believe, everyone wins—baby, mother, father, and the often-forgotten siblings.

Alternative parenting styles that suggest that all a mother has to do is open herself up to her baby's cues in order to form an attachment are missing half the equation. The difference here is profound. The cooperative parenting style as advocated by *Babywise,* recognizes that both baby and mom respond to cues—not just mom. It also operates from the premise that both mother and father are important in the child-rearing process. While mom may be the primary caregiver, dad is still part of the management team. Babies respond to all of this with healthy growth, healthy sleep, and the security of knowing they are loved.

What Will It Be for You?

Every parent wants to be a good mother or good father. This is satisfying and certainly socially acceptable. There was a time not long ago in our society when the success of a mother's influence was measured by the results of her labors, not the methods. The successful mother of the past proficiently managed her children, their day, and their behavior.

Today the rules have changed. Good mothering is often measured by the method of parenting rather than the results. Therefore, the definition of "good mother" has come to mean different things to different people. Where does that leave you? How do you choose which parenting route to take?

Because every philosophy of parenting has a corresponding pathology, we invite new and expectant parents to consider, evaluate, and decide which philosophy is best for their family. Review all the options. Examine carefully the alternative theories, approaches, and specifically *observe the end results.* Determine which parenting strategy is right for you, especially when it comes to infant nurturing.

Spend time with relatives and friends who follow the attachment-parenting style, hyperscheduling, and those who do *Babywise.* In which homes do you observe order, peace and tranquility? Observe the marriages as well as the children. Is mom in a perpetual state of exhaustion? Is dad sleeping on the couch? What is family life like when a child is six, twelve, and eighteen months? Is mom stressed, exhausted, frustrated or insecure. Is the baby stressed, exhausted, frustrated or insecure? Who is sleeping and where?

The best evaluation of any parenting philosophy, including *Babywise,* is not found in the reasoning or the logic of the hypothesis. End results speak clearly. Let your eyes confirm what works and what doesn't. You will be most confident in your parenting when you see the desired results lived out in other families.

Questions for Review

1. During this century, what were the two predominant views of infant management? What did they emphasize?

2. What is the birth-trauma theory? What does it require from a mother?

3. Explain the difference between attachment parenting and the theories of attachment?

4. In parenting, when does protection turn to overprotection.

5. Explain the following statement: "PDF is the center point between hyperscheduling on one extreme and attachment parenting on the other."

Chapter Three

Babies and Sleep

y, what a happy baby!" People are stopping you in the grocery store, at the bank, and coming up to you in the coffee shop. They can't get over the sweet contentment and playful giggles comprising your baby's demeanor. Your baby is alert to the surroundings, taking in each new set of features presenting themselves at close range. Are you merely lucky, or have you done the homework necessary to guide your baby in establishing habits resulting in bliss?

Surely you desire what's best for your baby. Every good parent does. As a mother, you also need what's best for you. A fatigued and weary mom simply cannot effectively meet her baby's needs or anyone else's, for that matter. Babies do not connect well with burned-out mothers. Parent-directed feeding (PDF) can prevent that.

From feeding time to waketime to naptime, PDF is a twenty-four-hour a day strategy designed to meet the baby's needs for outward structure in tandem with nurturing your little guy's developing emotions. At the same time, life becomes predictable for mom as well. That is because throughout the day and night the three basic activities; feeding, waketime and naptime, repeat themselves in rhythmic cycles. Routine leads to consistency, consistency leads to stabilization of each activity. As a result, the whole family is blessed by the order brought to the baby's day.

PDF builds confidence in mothers. Confidence comes when you know what to expect. Life becomes more predictable for mom; she can plan her day's activities knowing that her baby's needs will be met in an orderly and timely manner. Mom is also healthier as a result of feeding her baby on a routine. She has the time to get restful sleep and the exercise she needs. If a baby has siblings, a plan will allow mom and dad to have time they need as well. Everyone wins with PDF.

With PDF, feeding time, waketime, and naptime cycles are both routine and predictable. Though a routine is always predictable, what is predictable does not necessarily establish routine. For example, Chelsea's mom follows the principles of PDF. This means approximately the same amount of time passes from one feeding/wake/naptime event to the next. So interaction with baby is both predictable and routine, an important first step in establishing continuous nighttime sleep.

Marisa's mom is following AP-type demand-feeding. As a result, interaction with Marisa is very predictable. Marisa cries and her mother responds by offering her breast. However, this reaction is far from routine. The time lapse between nursing varies greatly. One hour may pass this time. Then three hours the next. Followed by thirty minutes. Then another hour. Although feeding Marisa is predictable, it is also very erratic. We believe such erratic interplay between caregiver and baby throughout the first several weeks prevents sleep/wake cycles from organizing. Marisa simply can't get it together and get in sync with the outside world.

To truly grasp the many benefits of an infant routine, you must first acknowledge two popular misconceptions. The first states that an infant routine detracts from meeting a baby's physical and emotional needs. This is a misguided assumption that schedules are incompatible with love, care, concern, and successful breast-feeding. Nothing could be more untrue. The second misconception is that an infant fed on demand will usually be happier, healthier, and generally more secure than one fed routinely. The inaccuracy of this last statement is revealed in the PDF plan.

More Than Just Feeding

For better or worse, parents are the greatest influence on a child's ability to sleep. Expecting babies and young children to sleep through the night is very realistic. But this all-important life skill is rarely achieved apart from parental guidance. Healthy, full-term babies typically are born with the capacity to achieve seven to eight hours of continuous nighttime sleep between seven and nine weeks. Whether or not your child achieves this is determined predominately by the philosophy you adopt for feeding.

Why the feeding philosophy? Because every philosophy and sub-philosophy of parenting has its own corresponding conclusions. A feeding philosophy represents more than just passing on nourishment to a baby; it represents a complex value system with its own set of expectations and beliefs about what is best for a child. These beliefs ultimately define and direct mothering responses. What a mother expects and anticipates her baby to need or achieve will influence what she can and will do with her baby. Mothering expectations direct mothering responses and those responses produce cause-and-effect behaviors. It is that simple.

That is why we believe parents should study the results of every parenting philosophy as much as they study the philosophy itself, then decide what approach is best for their family. Your approach to feeding (demand versus routine) will have a profound influence on your child's biological rhythms, ultimately affecting the establishment of healthy sleep patterns or sleep disturbances.

For example, mothers who follow the AP approach to parenting see completely different behavioral results than *Babywise* moms. That is because the philosophy drives expectations, expectations dictate methods, and methods bring about conclusions. One of the most apparent conclusions of the PDF approach is the establishment of stable nighttime sleep patterns. Chelsea, our PDF baby, will establish healthy and continuous nighttime sleep sometime between the seventh and ninth week. She will probably be sleeping ten hours a night by week twelve. Her cousin Marisa, on the other hand, will still be waking two or three times a night to snack. To her mother's dismay, this pattern is apt to continue for two very long years, with mutual discontentment.

A second characteristic of PDF babies is the outstanding payoff associated with a good night's sleep. These PDF babies are characterized by contentment, healthy growth, and optimal alertness. People on the street will remark on a *Babywise* baby's happiness. These parents typically are targets of astounding reviews for baby and with good reason. Their babies truly exude happiness. They are well rested, secure in their parents' love.

Putting Chelsea on a flexible routine benefits not only Chelsea but Chelsea's mom. Her mother soon learns what to expect. As life with baby becomes ever more predictable, she can plan the day's activities in confidence, knowing Chelsea's needs will be met. The result is a proactive style of parenting. Contrast this to reactive parenting, typically less than satisfactory to both parent and child.

Chelsea's mom feels healthier as a result of her established feeding routine. She gets uninterrupted, truly restful sleep. She doesn't suffer from fatiguing middle-of-the-night feedings that are extended into the second year. She even has time and energy for other important relationships with husband, parents, family, and friends. If Chelsea has siblings, the routine also will allow her mom and dad to give those children special time. Again, everyone wins with PDF.

Can It Really Happen?

Why some babies sleep through the night early on and others don't has long been the subject of debate and study. The theories range from simple to complex, from logical to bizarre. The inexperienced first-time mother usually arrives at a simplistic conclusion: "Every child is different. Some babies are born sleepers and others are not." They hope beyond hope to luck-out and be blessed with the former.

The behavioral clinician may suggest that a child's temperament is the determining influence on sleep patterns: "Some children are easier to handle by nature; some are more difficult." Others may suggest that the need of each child varies: "A high-need baby requires more nocturnal parental interaction; a low-need baby requires less." Although each statement contains a grain of truth, the statements themselves are outdated. Rest assured, you can and should expect your baby to learn the skill of sleep. Consider the following three facts:

Fact One:

Who wouldn't want a child to sleep through the night? It just makes sense. To increase your likelihood of success, establish your infant in a parent-guided feed/wake/sleep routine. The key to success lies in the order of these events. First comes feeding time for baby, followed by some waketime. Naptime concludes the sequence. This routine interaction with these three activities encourages healthy nighttime sleep patterns. After the first week following baby's birth, mother's job is to establish this sequence.

Many parents mistakenly reverse the last two events, allowing sleep to conclude a feeding. When baby wakes from a short nap, cranky and fussy but not necessarily hungry, parents shake their heads and pull their hair wondering what went wrong. This frustrating circumstance is easily eliminated when parents maintain the prescribed order. In contrast, allowing an infant to regulate his own life leads to the formation of nighttime sleep disturbances and poor sleep habits.

To achieve optimum sleep development, start with a basic feed/wake/nap routine. Since most babies do not have the ability to organize their own sleep into healthy patterns, parents must take the lead. Here is where parenting begins, with wise decisions in the best interest of your child. Consider the alternative. Is the parent's job simply to respond to an infant's demands? When, then, would this concept switch over to allow the parents to direct the child? Toddler years? Preteen or teen years? Hardly. By then you've missed the boat, and your child sails full speed ahead oblivious to fundamental skills like falling comfortably asleep alone. That's only the beginning.

Marisa's parents wrongly believe their baby should regulate her own routine and that their job is simply to respond. After all, a baby knows when she is hungry and when she is ready for sleep. Right? Well, no one would dispute that babies know when they are hungry. However, a problem arises because they are not capable of regulating their hunger patterns. They need parents to do this for them. Babies also know when they are tired, but they are not capable of establishing stable sleep/wake cycles on their own. Here the parent asserts guidance in place of an infant's inability to establish his or her own order.

Parent-directed feeding provides necessary guidance. It establishes for baby a rhythmic structure which helps hunger cycles synchronize with planned wake and sleep times. These principles work because they focus on the constant factors of baby's development. Baby's temperament, a huge variable from child to child, is not an issue in achieving fundamental skills. As Chelsea's mother provides daily interaction with her baby through predictable feed/wake/nap cycles, Chelsea's hunger and sleep/wake patterns first organize then stabilize. Mom's predictable interactions are time cues for Chelsea. These cues assist Chelsea in organizing her biological clock and responding appropriately.

Between seven and nine weeks, Chelsea's parents can expect her nighttime sleep cycles to be a continuous 7–8 hours. After three months of age, that time is extended to 9–11 hours each night. This nighttime sleep is in addition to her regular naptime during the day. This means bliss for everyone. Mother. Baby. Father. Siblings. Perhaps even the family pet.

Fact Two:

From birth onward, infant hunger patterns will either become stable and regular or move towards inconsistency. When infants are fed on the PDF plan, their hunger patterns stabilize. The reason for this is that the hunger mechanism (digestion and absorption) operates as if it has a metabolic memory reinforced by routine. If Chelsea's feeding periods are regular, she will establish a hunger metabolism that is stable and predictable. For example, if her mom feeds her at approximately 7:00 A.M., 10:00 A.M., 1:00 P.M., 4:00 P.M., 7:00 P.M., and 10:00 P.M., Chelsea's hunger synchronizes with those times. This happens only where feeding periods are routine. As a result of organizing and establishing healthy feeding patterns, babies automatically organize and establish patterns of optimal sleep.

In contrast, erratic feeding periods confuse an infant's young memory. If the parent's response to baby changes from day to day, even hour to hour, there is no chance for the hunger/wake/sleep mechanism to stabilize. Baby is confused, uncomfortable, perhaps insecure. This absence of routine for baby typically breeds unhealthy sleep patterns. No one seems to know what is expected. Least of all, baby.

Fact Three

It is not what goes in the mouth as much as when it goes in. Clearly there is a distinction between the sleep behavior of the AP child and that of the PDF child. Marisa has great difficulty establishing stable and uninterrupted nighttime sleep. Sometimes she wakes as often as every two hours on a recurring basis and she may do this routinely for two years, according to some studies.[1] This pattern is not healthy for Marisa or her mom. Fatigue soon sets in, and baby becomes cranky and difficult to sooth. Fatigue is further reinforced. Marisa's mom believes her daughter's inability to sleep continuously through the night is a result of breast-feeding. She read somewhere that breast-fed babies are not capable of sleeping through the night.

Failure to establish continuous nighttime sleep is not at all asso-ciated with breast- or bottle-feeding. When the feeding occurs, not what the feeding consists of, has much more to do with baby's healthy sleep. Mothers who demand-feed their babies with formula usually end up with the same unfortunate results experienced by moms who breast-feed on demand.

Chelsea and thousands of other breast-fed babies on PDF sleep through the night just fine, without disruption to lactation. Our sleep studies of 520 infants demonstrate that PDF breast-fed babies will sleep through the night on average at the same rates and in many cases slightly sooner than formula-fed babies (study details below.) This statistical conclusion dismantles the old wives' tale which attrib-uted nighttime sleep to a tummy full of formula. It also demonstrates that neither the composition of breast milk or formula, nor the speed in which the two are digested have any bearing on a child's ability to establish healthy nighttime sleep patterns.

Sleep/Wake Cycles

In the early months, an infant spends most of his or her time sleeping. This is good news for mom or so she thinks. Actually, the kind of sleep baby achieves determines its true value. You see, half of baby's sleep time necessarily is spent in quiet sleep (relaxed sleep pattern or RSP) and the other half in active sleep (active sleep pattern or ASP). Researchers tell us these two patterns should alternate about every thirty to forty-five minutes during sleep time.

Noticeable differences exist between these two patterns. During the relaxed sleep state, you see a peaceful baby. The baby's face is relaxed, eyelids closed and still. He or she has very few body movements and breathing is quiet and regular. On the other hand, the active sleep state is more restless. In both children and adults, this is our dream state. The extent to which infants dream is not yet known. However, during this period the arms and legs stir, the eyes and mouth flutter, and facial activities—such as sucking, frowning, and chewing motions—occur. Breathing is irregular and slightly faster.

Marisa is missing out on the deeper, quiet sleep her body requires. Although Marisa experiences some RSP, she fails to experience the cycle on a continual basis. From the start, she has been put to the breast ten to fifteen times a day and allowed to suckle for forty-five minutes to an hour. With that type of feeding pattern, there isn't much time left for the RSP cycle to repeat itself. Marisa's nights are much like her days, a series of naps between many feedings. Not so for Chelsea. Chelsea has learned to achieve the necessary length of sleep between feedings, enabling the RSP/ASP cycle to naturally repeat itself. For her, this sleep cycle is routine.

Statistical Norms for PDF Babies

What Can You Expect?

A child's body develops faster during the first year of life than any other time. To help facilitate healthy growth, a baby needs restful periods of sleep. The long standing debate is whether or not parents can help organize these sleep periods. The question has stumped researchers for a quarter of a century. We will confidently tell you that getting a baby to take good naps or sleep through the night consistently is not as difficult as the American public as been led to believe. While we cannot offer you any guarantees, we can offer you the following statistics that represent *Babywise* norms.

How do feedings distributed equally throughout the day affect nighttime sleep habits? Our study objective was to establish sleep norms for PDF participants. Conclusions were drawn from a convenient sampling of 520 infants (266 males, 254 females), of which 380 were exclusively breast-fed, 59 formula-fed, and 81 fed a combination of breast milk and formula. There were 468 babies with no medical conditions and 52 with some medical conditions detected at birth or shortly after birth. Included in the medical conditions profile were 15 premature infants. All parents followed a parent-directed feeding strategy.

Routine feedings for participants were defined as feeding newborns every 2 1/2 to 3 hours for the first eight weeks for breast-fed babies and every 3 to 4 hours for formula fed babies. Continuous nighttime sleep was defined as sleeping through the night 7–8 hours continuously. Volunteer subjects were drawn from the United States, Canada, and New Zealand. The study revealed the following:

Category: Exclusively Breast-fed Babies

Of the breast-fed girls, 86.9% were sleeping through the night between 7 and 9 weeks and 97% were sleeping through the night by 12 weeks.

Of the breast-fed boys, 76.8% were sleeping through the night between 7 and 9 weeks and 96% were sleeping though the night by 12 weeks.

Category: Exclusively Formula-fed Babies

Of the formula-fed girls, 82.1% were sleeping through the night between 7 and 9 weeks and 96.4% were sleeping through the night by 12 weeks.

Of the formula-fed boys, 78.3% were sleeping through the night between 7 and 9 weeks and 95.7% were sleeping through the night by 12 weeks.

Category Medical conditions

Of the 52 infants with medical conditions, (e.g. reflux, colic, premature infants, viro infections and unspecified hospitalization), all slept through the night 8–9 hours between 13 and 16 weeks.

As the percentages above demonstrate, parents can guide their baby's sleep/wake rhythms quite early and with a high degree of predictability. In addition, 80 percent of babies in our survey began sleeping through the night on their own—without any further parental guidance apart from routine feedings. It just happened. Some periods of night crying were experienced by the remaining 20 percent of children. Most of this took place over a three-day period and the crying bouts averaged between five and thirty-five minutes in the middle of the night. On average it took three to five days for a nine-week-old to break the old patterns of sleep and establish new ones.

Healthy Sleep Patterns

"How well did you sleep last night?" We all know about different levels of sleep. Yet few think to consider how well our wakefulness is. Did you know that there are different levels of wakefulness? Parents of infants especially tend to think only in terms of the two broadest categories, asleep or awake. While sleep ranges from a completely relaxed state to fitful rest, the awake state ranges from tiredness to optimal alertness. Most concerning is that optimal sleep is directly linked to optimal alertness. In turn, optimal alertness directly impacts optimal cognitive development. What role does healthy sleep play in the developmental process? Are you ready for this? Night sleepers make smarter children.

In his book *Healthy Sleep Habits, Happy Child,* Doctor Marc Weissbluth, Director of the Sleep Disorders Center at Children's Memorial Hospital in Chicago, references the work of Dr. Lewis M. Terman. Dr. Terman is best known for the Stanford-Binet Intelligence Test. His findings, published in 1925, on factors influencing IQ continue to stand unchallenged to this day, according to Weissbluth. His study looked at over three thousand children. In every age category, children who tested with superior intelligence had one common link: all of them had experienced healthy sleep at night.

In 1983, Dr. Terman's studies were objectively repeated by Canadian researchers and the same conclusions were reached. Children with healthy sleep patterns clearly had higher IQs than children who did not sleep well.[2]

Doctor Weissbluth not only speaks out on the positive aspects of healthy sleep but the negative aspects of disruptive sleep. He warns parents that "sleep problems not only disrupt a child's nights, they disrupt his days, too, (a) by making him less mentally alert, more inattentive, unable to concentrate, or easily distracted, and (b) by making him more physically impulsive, hyperactive, or alternatively lazy."[3]

Infants, pre-toddlers, and toddlers who suffer from the lack of healthy naps and continuous nighttime sleep may experience chronic fatigue. Fatigue is a primary cause of fussiness, daytime irritability, crankiness, discontentment, colic-like symptoms, hypertension, poor focusing skills and poor eating habits. In contrast, children who have established healthy sleep habits are optimally awake and optimally alert to interact with their environment. These children are self-assured and happy, less demanding, and more sociable. They have longer attention spans and, as a result, become faster learners.

Some researchers believe there is a cause and effect relationship with poor sleep habits and the rate of attention deficit hyperactive disorder (ADHD). According to the National Institute of Mental Health, ADHD affects two million or 5 percent of children in the United States. The title is applied to children diagnosed with learning disabilities, hyperactive behavior, poor focusing and concentrating skills, and those lacking the basic skill of paying attention.

With thousands of PDF children around the country, we were curious to know what the ADHD rates were among the PDF population. To find out, we conducted a preliminary retrospective survey of 423 school children five years and older, all who during infancy established healthy naps and nighttime sleep habits as outlined in *Babywise*. Of the 423 children, only six children (.014%) carried the ADHD label. Surprisingly low as these results may be, they do make sense. Healthy sleep positively effects neurologic development and appears to be the right medicine for the prevention of many learning and behavioral deficiencies.

Is Infant Sleep Deprivation Dangerous?

Imagine your spouse getting no more than three hours sleep at a stretch for one week. Would you expect this to impact his or her attitudes, actions, and overall accountability? Certainly the negative effects on his or her mature central nervous system are widely known. You would not be surprised to observe your partner becoming irritable and weak, having difficultly concentrating, perhaps experiencing partial neurologic shutdown. This is just the beginning. Now consider an infant whose central nervous system is still developing. Even more is at stake. To what extent, then, does sleep deprivation negatively impact an infant's developing central nervous system?

Imagine parenting in such a way that your baby is not allowed to sleep continuously for eight hours for even one night out of three hundred and sixty-five. Is it possible that many of the learning disabilities associated with nonstructured parenting are rooted in something as basic as sleep? As the higher brain continues developing during the first year of life, a definite possibility exists that the absence of continuous nights of sleep are harmful to this process.

Sleep Props Hinder Continuous Nighttime Sleep

The typical infant has both the natural ability and the capacity to sleep through the night sometime within the first nine weeks of life. It is an acquired skill which is enhanced by routine. Sleep deprivation in infants and toddlers has much less to do with nature than with nurture. Since sleep is a natural function of the body, the primary cue for infant sleep is sleepiness.

Sleep cues are influenced (often negatively) by a variety of sleep association props. Some sleep props, such as a special blanket or a stuffed animal, are harmless, while others are addictive. For some parents, the problem is getting the child to fall asleep initially. For others, the challenge is getting the child to fall back to sleep without a prop once he or she is prematurely awakened. Let's examine three of the most common negative sleep props.

- Intentionally nursing a baby to sleep
- Rocking a baby to sleep
- Sleeping with your baby (shared sleep)

Intentionally Nursing Your Baby to Sleep

The scenario is all too familiar. A mother nurses her baby to sleep. Slowly raising herself from the chair, she eases toward the crib. While holding her breath, she gently lowers the precious bundle and allows herself to smile. Then, frozen in time, she anxiously awaits peace to settle over the crib before backing to the door. She wonders, what will it be? Freedom or failure? Hoping to escape, mother knows if baby fusses it's "take it from the top time," and she begins the process again.

Parents don't need to be in bondage to their baby's sleep needs. The question certainly is not whether you should nurse your baby. Rather, is nursing appropriate for inducing sleep each time sleep is needed? We say no. The practice of nursing the baby to sleep creates an unnecessary dependency on mom for sleep. This prevents baby from learning how to achieve sleep on his or her own. With the PDF plan your baby will establish healthy sleep patterns. When baby is placed in the crib, he or she is awake. No tiptoeing, breath-holding, or freeze maneuvers required.

Rocking Your Baby to Sleep

First came the rocking chair. Then the clothes dryer. Then the car. This is not a litany of luxuries, but lullabies. Modern mechanical sleep props like placing baby on top of a running clothes dryer (really!) or taking baby for a cruise in the family van are similar to old-fashioned chair rocking. Each relies on specific stimulation to lull baby to sleep, either initially or after waking prematurely.

Again, this is not about whether you should rock or cuddle your baby. We trust that happens regularly. But are you using rocking as a sleep prop that interferes with your child learning to fall asleep? Similar to rocking a baby to sleep are a host of mechanical props. For example, someone discovered that if a baby is placed in an infant seat on top of an operating dryer, the dryer will create enough vibration to lull the baby to sleep. This is not a safe or wise practice. Another method is the naptime or nighttime car ride. In this scenario, the sound of the motor and the vibrating chassis of the car sends baby to lullaby land. Both approaches sometimes work, albeit temporarily. That is, they work until the dryer runs out of time, the car runs out of gas, or you run out of patience.

Sleeping with Your Baby

Sharing sleep with children puts them at risk both physically and emotionally. According to the American Academy of Pediatrics, bed sharing may actually increase the risk of SIDS.[4] See chapter 11 for an expanded discussion on the dangers of shared sleep. Emotionally, it may create a state of abnormal dependency on the sleep prop to the point where the child actually fears falling asleep when transitioned to his or her own bed. As the child moves into toddlerhood, that fear is expressed through the need for mom or dad to lie down with the child at naptime until sleep is achieved. This not only robs parents of healthy sleep, the child also misses out on good rest.

The most serious sleep problems we've encountered are associated with parents who sleep with their babies. Researchers at the University of Massachusetts Medical School say co-sleeping may "prevent, rather than ensure, a good night's sleep." They studied 303 parents and their sleeping patterns. Families where co-sleeping occurred were more likely to have sleep problems with their children including night walking and difficulty falling asleep. High levels of sleeping problems remained with frequent co-sleeping families one year after the initial interview, suggesting that early co-sleeping fosters long term problems. Not only do children encounter long term sleep disruptions, but frequently the husband removes himself from the bed so he can get a good night's sleep.[5]

Why choose a prop? Instead, confidently establish a basic routine to naturally and beautifully enhance restful sleep. Put your baby to bed while both of you are still awake. In this way, baby will establish longer and stronger sleep cycles than if placed in the crib already asleep. Besides, none of the sleep props listed above offer any healthy advantages. Instead, carefully consider the long-term negative effects of sleep props. Vow to avoid them now, and you avoid creating behaviors that later need retraining. You'll have plenty to do without this unnecessary strain. Feed your baby, rock him and love him, but put him down before he falls asleep.

Questions for Review

1. How and why do feeding philosophies impact nighttime sleep?

2. How important is the order of events when it comes to establishing nighttime sleep?

3. Should you allow your baby to regulate his or her own routine? Explain your answer.

4. How do erratic feedings confuse an infant's young memory?

5. What is a "sleep prop"?

6. List three negative sleep props which hinder nighttime sleep.
   a.
   b.
   c.

Chapter Four

Facts
on Feeding

*C*uddles, kisses, and consistency. To baby, these are a few of his favorite things. Add in proper nutrition, and you are on the path to parenting success. Whether the nourishment comes from a bottle or breast, only you can choose. Both are discussed here for your knowledge and heartfelt deliberation. No matter what your choice, know that successful lactation alone, like raindrops on roses, will not deliver perfection in parenting. There is much more to good mothering than just bringing a baby to the breast.

Feeding your baby is perhaps the most basic task of managing your infant. Since a baby's sucking and rooting reflexes are well developed at birth, he will satisfy those reflexes by rooting and sucking on anything near his mouth. Whether feeding is accomplished by a bottle or the breast is not nearly as important as the gentle, tender cuddling you give him during feeding. Your decision to bottle- or breast-feed must be free of any coercion or manipulation. Guilt or a quest for approval is never in line with clear thinking. Instead, confidently base your decision on accurate, honest information.

Nothing beats breast-feeding for physiological benefits to baby. That's plain fact. Mother's milk is the complete and perfect food, nothing short of miraculous. Easily digested, it provides excellent nutrition and contains the right balance of proteins and fats. It also provides the additional antibodies necessary for building your baby's immune system.[1]

According to the American Academy of Pediatrics, there is strong evidence that breast milk decreases the incidence and or severity of diarrhea, lower respiratory infection, bacterial meningitis, and urinary tract infection.[2] The Academy also points out various studies demonstrating breast milk's protection against Sudden Infant Death Syndrome, allergic diseases, Crohn's disease, ulcerative colitis, and other chronic digestive diseases.[3]

There's more good news. Unlike formula which needs to be prepared, stored, warmed and packed for every outing, breast milk is always ready, whenever and wherever you go. And you never need wonder about the milk's freshness. Inside mother, it won't go bad. Breast-feeding has many health benefits for mom as well, such as helping to speed the return of the uterus to its normal size and shape. It also decreases the risk of breast cancer and facilitates easier postpartum weight loss. What new mother isn't eager to get back into pre-pregnancy clothes.

Breast-feeding Trends

Despite the numerous benefits of breast-feeding, the American Academy of Pediatrics notes that the number of mothers opting to breast-feed are lower than expected: "Although breast-feeding rates have increased slightly since 1990, the percentage of women currently electing to breast-feed their babies is still lower than levels reported in the mid-1980s and is far below the Healthy People 2000 goal," says the AAP. "In 1995, 59.4% of women in the United States were breast-feeding exclusively or in combination with formula-feeding at the time of hospital discharge; only 21.6% of mothers were nursing at six months, and many of these were supplementing with formula." The goal of Healthy People 2000 is to increase the number of breast-feeding mothers to 75% and to increase to 50% the number who will continue breast-feeding until their babies are five to six months old.[4]

Why do nearly half of all mothers choose against the nourishment, convenience, and physical closeness of breast-feeding? Why do over half of all mothers who initially choose breast-feeding opt out so early on? Are they simply callous women, cold to the nourishment and nurture of their babies, more concerned with freedom than baby's physical well-being? Of course not. There is more to their choice and change of heart than perceived on the surface. Quite possibly the decision to quit breast-feeding actually is a disturbing necessity for distraught and fatigued moms unable to cope with endless demands created by a faulty parenting philosophy.

The PDF moms reveal an interesting twist on the breast-feeding story. A convenient sampling of over 240 mothers following the PDF principles demonstrated that 88% of mothers who start with the program breast-feed, and 80% of those moms breast-feed exclusively with no formula supplement. And while the national average was 21.6% of mothers breast-feeding into the fifth month, a full 70% of PDF mothers continued into the fifth and six month. On the average, PDF moms breast-feed 33.2 weeks. Add to these statistics the benefits of uninterrupted nighttime sleep and you will better appreciate the wonderful benefits of a flexible routine.

For PDF mothers, there's no questioning or second-guessing what will happen next and when. The routine for these moms provides greater understanding of their babies' needs and helps them connect with their baby sooner. If problems occur, they typically fall so far outside a baby's normal pattern of behavior that mother quickly picks up on this distress. Breast-feeding under these conditions is delightful, not demanding.

But even with these wonderful statistics, transforming a woman into a good mother is one thing breast-feeding cannot do. There is no "good mother" hormone, and much more is required than just bringing a baby to breast. While strong support for breast-feeding does exist, no one should choose breast-feeding at all costs. The well-being of your entire family also is a critical consideration. Although breast milk is a significant link to the physical well-being of a baby, the act of breast-feeding itself is not the genesis of baby's psychological health. It is not a silver bullet assuring a love attachment or security.

If you want to ensure optimal development, provide a predictable routine for your baby. It will best complement baby's overall advancement and attachment in *all* critical areas of development. Combine this with breast-feeding and you truly can offer a total package for baby.

Is There Really a Difference?

Demand-feeding's more standard, moderate approach as used by Julia and Barbara introduced in chapter two, instructs parents to feed their babies every two to three hours based on the baby's hunger signals. On the other hand, PDF parents will feed their babies on a flexible routine every two to three hours. In terms of nutrition, both methods are the same. But as demonstrated earlier, the physiological outcomes are drastically different because one method is child led and the other parent directed.

As stated in chapter two, *Babywise* offers an alternative to hyper-scheduling on one extreme, and the AP style of nursing at the other. It has enough structure to bring security and order to your baby's world, yet it has enough flexibility to give mom freedom to respond to any need at anytime.

Some moms rely too heavily on watching and waiting for their baby to signal a desire to nurse. They may be discouraged when their babies nurse irregularly or want to nurse every hour. These mothers may worry about their baby getting enough food. The expectation that a baby should nurse *whenever* usually leads to frustration for both mother and baby and may be the single greatest reason mothers give up breast-feeding so quickly.

Waiting on the baby's signal for food may also compromise the child's health. Some newborns may not cry to signal hunger readiness for five or six hours, and crying is not always a signal of hunger. Weak and sickly babies may not have the energy to cry, so the advice to sit back and let the baby direct the show could allow serious medical problems to go unnoticed that would otherwise be picked up through routine feedings.[5] It is the predictability within the routine that helps PDF moms pick up any deviation from the norm. Deviation cues stand out because there is a pattern of normal cues.

"Just listen to your baby's cues" is common breast-feeding advice and good advice if you know what to listen and look for. Babies provide parents two sets of response cues. Those that are *immediate need cues,* (e.g. hunger, sleep, messy diaper cues), and those that represent a *parenting style.* Behavior patterns can be attributed to parenting styles as much as temperament. For example, the three-month-old baby who has a pattern of waking two, three, or four times in the middle of the night to nurse is responding to his mother's parenting style. In this case, the need cue for food may be legitimate, but the greater question centers on the greater parenting style cue—why is the child of this age repeatedly hungry at night? Mothers will say, "But my baby is waking for comfort nursing not just food." We would still ask the same question at this age. A baby nursing for comfort so many times during the night is a cue that your parenting style during the day is causing too much discomfort.

A baby nursing every hour is another double cue. It may signal that your baby is not getting the rich high-caloried hindmilk, and equally important, that your baby is not getting enough healthy sleep. Healthy sleep facilitates healthy nursing. Fatigue is another parenting style cue. If mom is continually waking up each morning fatigued and discouraged from her middle of the night experience, that is her body and emotion's way of telling her that what she is doing is not working.

In contrast, the baby who is growing and sleeping contently and securely through the night is also responding to a parenting style. This is a healthy response signaling that tummies are content as well as hearts. What about the Mom who wakes in the morning feeling rested? That sense of restedness is a positive response cue to what she is doing. Parents must learn how to distinguish between immediate need cues and parenting style cues—both are important. One for short-term benefit and one for long-term gain.

Milk Production

If breast-feeding is your choice, there are a few basic principles you must understand. Most important is that breast-feeding success is based on demand and supply. The supply of milk produced by the glands is proportional to the demand placed on the system. The greater the demand, the greater the supply. But how do you define demand?

Marisa's mother heard that milk production is directly related to the number of feedings offered. The more feedings she gave, the greater would be her milk production. While there is some truth here, the statement is greatly misleading. Certainly a mother who takes her baby to breast seven times a day will produce more milk than the one who offers only two feedings. However, there are limits. A mother who takes her baby to her breast twelve, fifteen, or twenty times a day will not necessarily produce any more milk than the mom who takes her baby to breast eight or nine times a day.

The problem isn't the amount of milk overall, but the quality of the milk taken in by baby. First, babies on a routine of fewer feedings will take in more calories at each of those set feedings than babies who feed ad lib.[6] The difference here is qualitative feeding, as with a baby on a routine; versus quantitative feeding, meaning more feedings at lesser quality.

With qualitative feeding, you eliminate the need for continual snacking. Many feedings become exactly that. Baby feels like a little something to tide her over. No meal is desired. Such snack feeding provides baby only a partial meal consisting of the lower-calorie *foremilk* and not the higher-calorie *hindmilk* essential for growth. Mom thinks she's doing more for baby through endless breast availability. In actuality, she's delivering less than her best. Baby often quits suckling before optimum nourishment is offered. How disheartening for both.

Part of a mother's ability to produce milk is tied to the demand placed on her system. Several factors are associated with the demand side of breast-milk production, with two being specific to this discussion. First, there is the need for appropriate stimulation at each feeding. That means the strength of the infant's suck must be sufficient.[7] A second factor for the PDF baby is the correct amount of time between feedings. Without proper stimulation, no matter how many times an infant goes to the breast, milk production will be limited. Too many snack feedings, with too little time in between, may reduce proper stimulation. Thus, baby gets only foremilk, much lower in calories than the most desirable hindmilk. Too few feedings, allowing too much time in between feedings, reduces mother's milk production. Both proper time lapse and stimulation are needed for breast-feeding success.

References to breast stimulation refer to intensity of baby's sucking. The urgency of baby's hunger drive consistently will influence the sucking reflex. This drive for food is related to the time needed for milk digestion and absorption into baby's system. An infant fed on a basic 2½ to 3 hour routine and whose digestive metabolism is stable, will demand more milk. In turn, this stimulates greater milk production than the infant demanding less milk more often. Here then lies your key to efficient milk production. Work on getting full feedings.

The Let-Down Reflex

When a baby begins to suckle on his mother's breast, a message is sent to the mother's pituitary gland, which in turn releases several hormones. The hormone prolactin is necessary for milk production, and the hormone oxytocin is required for milk release. The most important factor in the continued release of prolactin is proper nipple stimulation. Without this stimulation, milk will not be produced no matter how many times an infant goes to the breast. A consistent routine will help maximize milk production.

Before the milk is let down, your baby will receive a milk substance stored in the ducts under the areola (the flesh encircling the nipples). This foremilk, as it is called, is diluted and limited in nutritional value. Oxytocin then causes the cells around the milk glands to contract, forcing milk into the ducts. When that happens, the milk is said to have been let down. For some mothers, this experience includes a tingling or pressure sensation. Without let-down, the milk would remain in the glands. In the absence of any sensation, the most reliable sign of let-down is your baby's rhythmic swallowing of milk. The milk released is called hindmilk or mature milk. This high-protein and high-fat-content milk is rich in calories (thirty to forty per ounce).

Mothers following PDF have little or no problem with the let-down reflex. There are two reasons for this. First, routine plays an important part in proper let-down. Not only does the mind need a routine to maintain order and efficiency, but the body does as well. The very nature of inconsistent feeding wears on a woman's body. A second reason is the high confidence level of the mother who follows a routine. There is no worrisome fear or anxiety for moms who know what happens next. Mother is confident, and her confidence aids the successful working of her let-down reflex.

Breast Milk and Baby's Digestion

An empty stomach does not trigger the hunger drive. Efficient and effective digestion and absorption of food does. This is where the various food groups get broken down into proteins, fats, and carbohydrates. After the breakdown, the nutrition is assimilated into the body via the blood. Absorption, which takes place primarily in the small intestine, is the process by which broken-down food molecules pass through the intestinal lining into the bloodstream. As absorption is accomplished, the blood-sugar level drops, sending a signal to the hypothalamus gland. The red-alert is triggered: baby now needs food. So it is blood sugar dropping, not the empty tummy, which signals feeding time.

Breast milk is digested faster than formula, but that doesn't justify unlimited breast-feedings to try and play catch-up. Rather than comparing breast milk to formula, it's more useful to look at the amount of breast milk consumed at each feeding. The AP style of demand-feeding does not distinguish been snack time and mealtime. For these mothers, a feeding is a feeding. The child who nurses frequently and takes in fewer ounces, especially of foremilk, will naturally be hungry more often. PDF moms look to deliver full meals at each feeding.

Proper Position for Nursing Your Baby

During the first few days of nursing, find a comfortable position for baby and you. This may be a matter of personal preference or an eclectic assortment based on situational needs. A pillow may be helpful under your supporting arm to lessen stress on your neck and upper back. Correct positioning of your precious bundle is imperative in successful lactation. Also, how comfortable you are with this experience is directly affected by the angles you impose on baby and yourself.

With your nipple, stroke lightly downward on your baby's lower lip until she opens her mouth. Take care not to touch her upper lip as this creates confusion for baby. As her mouth opens wide, center your nipple and pull her close to you so that the tip of her nose is brushing slightly against your breast and her knees are resting on your abdomen. With baby correctly latched on, nursing should not be painful. Successful latching is made difficult if the baby's head is toward the breast but the body is allowed to turn away. If there is discomfort, remove her and try again. Patience in the process pays off as you discover what's best for you both.

When the baby nurses, she should take both the nipple and all or much of the areola into her mouth. Encourage the baby to latch on to the areola, though she may seem satisfied with only the nipple. Also, see that your baby's entire body is facing you (head, chest, stomach, and legs). She will not latch on correctly if her head is facing you but the rest of her body isn't. While this may sound awkward and impossible, baby has only one thing in mind when approaching the breast. Ideal positioning is not an issue for her consideration. You need to take charge here.

A nursing baby often has a remarkably strong suck. If you try to pull the nipple away, she will just suckle harder. Just once interrupt a feeding suddenly to answer the door and you will quickly discover baby's intensity in this area. It's a lesson that endures. To remove her without hurting yourself, slip your little finger between the corner of her mouth and your breast. That will break the intense suction, allowing you to take her off easily. To further assist in achieving successful feeding, there are three correct and interchangeable nursing positions: Cradle, side-lying, and football hold.

Cradle Position

The cradle position is most common. Sitting in a comfortable position, place your baby's head in the curve of your arm. You may desire to place a pillow under your supporting arm to lessen the stress on your neck and upper back. When the baby nurses, he should take both the nipple and all or much of the areola into his mouth. Encourage and assist the baby in latching on to the areola. With this approach, your baby's entire body should face you (head, chest, stomach and legs). Again, he will not latch on correctly if his head is  facing you, but the rest of his body is not. With your nipple, stroke lightly downward on his lower lip until he opens his mouth. When his mouth opens wide, center your nipple and pull him close to you so the tip of his nose is touching your breast and his knees are touching your abdomen.

Side-lying position

This position is commonly used by moms recovering from a cesarean delivery. Your stomach and your baby's stomach should be facing, and your baby's head is near the nipple. With your nipple, stroke lightly downward on his lower lip until he opens his mouth. When his mouth opens wide, center your nipple and pull him close to you so the tip of his nose is touching your breast.

Football hold

The football hold finds one hand under the infant's head pulling him close. The breast is lifted and supported by the other hand. With the fingers above and below the nipple, introduce the baby to the breast by drawing him near. As explained above, stroke lightly downward on baby's lower lip until he opens his mouth. When his mouth opens wide, center your nipple and pull him close to you so the tip of his nose is touching your breast.

How Often Should I Nurse My Baby?

How often you should feed your baby depends on baby's age. As a general rule, during the first two months you will feed your baby approximately every $2^1/2$ to 3 hours from the beginning of one feeding to the beginning of the next. Sometimes it may be less and sometimes slightly more, but this time frame is a healthy average. In actual practice, a $2^1/2$-hour routine means you will nurse your baby two hours from the end of the last feeding to the start of the next, adding back in twenty to thirty minutes for feeding to complete the cycle. A three-hour routine means you will nurse your baby $2^1/2$ hours from the end of the last feeding to the start of the next. When you add twenty to thirty minutes for the actual feeding time, you will complete your three-hour cycle. With these recommended times you can average between eight to ten feedings a day in the early weeks. These times fall well within recommendations of the American Academy of Pediatrics.[8]

While $2^1/2$- to 3-hour feedings are a healthy norm, there may be occasions when you might feed sooner. But take heed. Consistently feeding exclusively at $1^1/2$- to 2-hour intervals may wear a mother down. Extreme fatigue reduces her physical ability to produce a sufficient quantity and even quality of milk. Add postpartum hormones to the mix and it isn't any wonder some women simply throw in the towel. Bear in mind, the word *consistently* is operative. As stated, there will be times when you might nurse sooner than $2^1/2$ hours, but that should not be the norm. At the other extreme, going longer than $3^1/2$ hours in the early weeks can produce too little stimulation for successful lactation.

The First Milk

The first milk produced is a thick, yellowish liquid called colostrum. Colostrum is at least five times as high in protein as mature milk with less fat and sugar. As a protein concentrate, it takes longer to digest and is rich in antibodies. Some mothers experience tenderness in the first few days before mature milk comes in. This is due to the thickness of the colostrum and the infant sucking especially hard to remove it. A typical pattern is suck, suck, suck, then swallow. When mature milk becomes available, your baby responds with a rhythmic suck, swallow, suck, swallow, suck, swallow. At that point, the hard sucking is reduced and the tenderness should dissipate.

A clicking sound and dimpled cheeks during nursing are two indicators that your baby is not sucking adequately. Take the following test yourself. Curl your tongue and place it near the roof of your mouth and then pull it away. You should hear a clicking sound. When your baby is nursing, your should *not* hear that sound nor see dimpled cheeks. It means your baby is sucking his own tongue not the breast. If you hear clicking remove baby from breast and then relatch him. If this continues, contact your pediatrician.

Even with a complete understanding of how the breast works and the many benefits of colostrum, mothers may still wonder if their babies are getting enough food in that first week. Consider these important clues. One sign that your baby is receiving adequate nutrition is his stooling pattern. Newborn stools in the first week transition from meconium, greenish black and sticky in texture, to a brownie batter transition stool, to a sweet-odor, mustard yellow stool. The yellow stool is a totally breast-milk stool and a healthy sign. After the first week, two to five or more yellow stools along with seven to eight wet diapers daily are healthy signs that your baby is getting adequate milk to grow on. Healthy baby growth indicators are discussed in chapter 5. A bottle-fed baby will pass firmer, light brown to golden- or clay-colored stools, strong in odor.

After Your Milk Comes In

Unless specified by your pediatrician, a baby normally does not need additional water or formula prior to mother's milk coming in because your baby is getting colostrum. Once your milk is in, your nursing periods will average fifteen minutes per side. As mentioned, some babies nurse faster, some slower. Studies show that in established lactation, a baby can empty the breasts in seven to ten minutes per side, providing he or she is sucking vigorously. This astounding truth is not meant to encourage less time at the breast. Rather, it's a clear demonstration of baby's ability for speed and efficiency.

Under normal circumstances, baby takes what's needed within thirty minutes. The idea that non-nutritive sucking beyond this time enhances a baby's security or heightens a baby's sense of love is interesting but lacks serious scientific support. Security and love result from the overall parent-child relationship, not one isolated factor. If you feel your baby has a need for non-nutritive sucking, a pacifier can meet the need without compromising your routine. But even with this, be careful not to overuse the pacifier.

Usually a woman's milk comes in between three and six days. During that period, some weight loss in the baby (up to 10 percent of birth weight) is normal and expected but should be regained in ten to fourteen days. In his practice, Dr. Bucknam recommends that babies be weighed at ten to fourteen days of life. If there is a problem, it will show up on the scales. Catching it early is easy to correct and obviously much safer. Weight gain, as well as three to five or more yellow stools daily for the first month and five to seven wet diapers per day after the first week, are good indicators that your baby is getting enough milk for healthy growth.

Nursing Periods

Current wisdom governing the length of nursing periods for the first few days is fairly consistent. We suggest the following:

The Very First Nursing Period

If possible, nurse your baby soon after birth. This will be sometime within the first hour and a half when newborns usually are the most alert. We suggest you strive for fifteen minutes per side or a minimum of ten minutes per side. Remember to properly position the baby on the breast. If your baby wants to nurse longer during this first feeding, allow him or her to do so. In fact, with the first several feedings you can go as long as the two of you are comfortable. Both breasts need to be stimulated at each feeding, and the initial time frame mentioned above will allow for sufficient breast stimulation.

The First Five Days

Throughout the next three to five days, maintain your basic $2^1/2$- to 3-hour routine, nursing fifteen to twenty minutes on each breast. This means your average nursing period falls between thirty and forty minutes per feeding during this first week. Babies are usually sleepy during the first several days after birth. As a result, some will fall asleep right at the breast after a few minutes of nursing. That means you may have to work on keeping your baby awake at the breast. (Rub his feet, stroke his face, change a diaper, talk to him, remove his sleeper, but he must eat.) Keeping him awake will help him take in full feedings as opposed to snacking. It's your key to success, both in terms of early lactation and establishing a healthy routine. In our experience, mothers who work to get a full feeding during the first week have a baby who naturally transitions into a consistent three-hour routine within seven to ten days. Keep this goal in mind when putting in the extra effort. The payoff comes in confidence and comfort for both baby and you.

Some mothers nurse fifteen to twenty minutes on each side, burping their baby before switching breasts. Other mothers find it helpful to employ a ten-ten-five-five method. They alternate, offering each breast for ten minutes (burping the baby between sides), and then offer each breast for five additional minutes. This second method is especially helpful when you have a sleepy baby. The disruption prompts your baby to wakefulness and assures that both breasts are stimulated. Please note that these figures are goals based on an average. Some newborns nurse faster and more efficiently. Others nurse efficiently but slightly slower. If your baby wants to nurse longer let him do so.

Jaundice in Newborns

A mild degree of jaundice is common in most newborns. This is not a disease but a temporary condition characterized by a yellow tinge to the skin and eyes. Jaundice, caused by the pigment bilirubin in the blood, is usually easily controlled. However, it could develop into a dangerous situation if ignored or left untreated. If the condition appears more pronounced after the second day, frequent blood tests are done and conservative treatment initiated.

Babies with moderately raised levels of bilirubin are sometimes treated with special fluorescent lights that help to break down the yellow pigment. Also part of treatment is an increase in fluid intake. In this case your pediatrician may recommend other liquid supplements although exclusive breast-feeding is usually the best way to correct this condition, even feeding as often as every two hours. Because billirubin is eliminated in the stool, make sure your baby has passed his first stool (meconium). Your doctor will determine the program of treatment best suited for your baby. Because a newborn with jaundice will tend to sleep more, be sure to wake your baby for feeding at least every 3 hours.

Breast Versus Bottle

We know the nutritional and health benefit disparity between breast milk and formula over the first twelve weeks of baby's life is substantial. By six months of age, this disparity remains. However, it is to a lesser degree than in the first twelve weeks. According to the American Academy of Pediatrics, this six month term is the minimum recommended duration. Between six and nine months, the difference between what is best and what is good continues to narrow. That is partly due to the fact that other food sources are now introduced in your baby's diet. Between nine and twelve months, the nutritional value of breast milk drops and food supplements are usually needed. Going beyond a year in our society is done more out of a preference for nursing than an absolute nutritional need.

When it comes to nourishing baby, mother's milk is clearly superior to formula. Now for the stickier issue of nurturing. Is breast superior to bottle? In times past, experts said yes. Stressing the value of breast-feeding, they associated bottle-feeding with child rejection. Considered to be lacking warmth, a bottle-feeding mom was accused of renouncing her biological role as a woman and her emotional role as a mother. Others considered bottle-fed children to have less of an advantage in life than those who were breast-fed. In truth, studies over the last sixty years which attempted to correlate method of infant feeding with later emotional development failed to support any of these conclusions. A mother's overall attitude toward her child far outweighs any single factor, including manner of feeding.

Bottle Feeding

Bottle-feeding is not a twentieth-century discovery, but a practice in existence for thousands of years. Our ancestors made bottles out of wood, porcelain, pewter, glass, copper, leather, and cow horns. Historically, unprocessed animal's milk was the principal nourishment used with bottle-feeding. Since this milk was easily contaminated, infant mortality was high.

During the first half of this century, when bottle-feeding was in vogue, selection was relatively limited. Not so today. Your grocer's shelves are filled with options. Besides the standard glass and plastic bottles, there are those with disposable bags, designer imprints, handles and animal shapes. All of these come in a clever range of colors and prints. This perhaps is more for mother's amusement than baby's. Adding to the confusion is a varied selection of supposedly proper nipples. You can find everything from a nursing nipple that is most like mom to an orthodontic nipple. There are juice, formula, water and even cereal nipples, so baby can suckle her table food. With so many choices, don't go to the store without adequate rest.

In truth, the most important consideration is making sure you purchase a nipple with the right-sized hole. That's it. With too large a hole, the child drinks too fast. Excessive spitting up and projectile vomiting can be signs of too-rapid fluid intake. Remembering this simple tip can save you many a midnight mop-up. Conversely, a hole which is too small creates a hungry and discontented child. Imagine the frustration! These simple tips will prevent what could be major feeding problems for your baby and you.[9]

One advantage to bottle-feeding is it allows others to participate. Feeding time for dad is just as special for him as for mom. Fathers should not be denied this opportunity to nurture. The same holds true for age-appropriate siblings and grandparents. It's a family affair. All participants, especially baby, benefit with this family approach.

Formula

Take time to sit and hold your baby while feeding with a bottle. What better time to sneak in the rest you deserve, not to mention the cuddling your baby requires. Holding your baby at this time will also help prevent your child from becoming attached to the bottle. You control the feeding with the bottle in your hands. Not baby.

Generally, avoid feeding baby while he or she is lying completely flat, such as when the mother is nursing in the lying-down position. Swallowing while lying down may allow fluid to enter the middle ear, leading to ear infections. For the same reason, avoid propping up the bottle. Putting a child six months and older to bed with a bottle is a no-no. This is true not only for health factors relating to ear infections but also for oral hygiene. When a child falls asleep with a bottle in his mouth, the sugar in the formula remaining in the mouth coats the teeth. Tooth decay results.

Most important in bottle-feeding is what goes in the bottle. Sometimes the choice may be made for you either by the hospital where you deliver or by your pediatrician. If either your husband or you have a history of milk allergies, mention that to your doctor. It may influence the type of formula your pediatrician recommends. Formulas today have properties closely matched to those of breast milk, including the proper balance and quantity of proteins, fats, and carbohydrates. Cow's milk and baby formula are not the same. Formula is designed for a baby's digestive system; cow's milk is not. Cow's milk is not suitable for children less than one year old. For more specific information regarding the different manufacturers of formula, check with your pediatrician.

The amount of formula taken at each feeding will vary with the baby's age. On average, as with breast-fed babies, it is anywhere from 1 1/2 to 3 ounces per feeding in the first several weeks. This amount gradually increases as baby grows. If you prepare a four-ounce bottle for each feeding and allow your baby to take as much as he or she wants, the baby will tend to stop when full. While a larger baby might take more milk, that is not always the case. As with breast-fed babies, the feeding routine is what establishes the corresponding hunger patterns. Not the substance or the amount of food.

Again, we can not overstate breast milk's advantage in infant nourishment. However, if you choose not to nurse, you can't nurse, or if you decide to discontinue nursing within the first twelve months, the decision will not make you an unloving mother. Just as breast-feeding doesn't make you a good mother, bottle-feeding won't make you a bad one.

Burping Your Baby

Baby needs to burp. Initially, formula-fed babies must be burped every one-half ounce. By the time your baby is four to six months old, he or she will probably be able to consume six to eight ounces before burping. With both breast-feeding and bottle-feeding, there is a certain amount of spitting up. You'll learn to expect it. (For more on spitting up see page 205.) However, if you find your infant rejecting all his food frequently, put in a call to your pediatrician.

Here are several workable techniques to assist in burping your baby to bliss.

1. Place the palm of your hand over baby's stomach.

Figure 4.1

Now hook your thumb around the side of your baby, wrapping the rest of your fingers around the chest area. Your hand should be baby's only support. You may rest the baby's bottom on your knee, but allow all of the baby's weight to be placed on your supporting hand. Next, lean the baby over your hand. If the baby is wiggling or needs further support, you may hold his or her hands in your supporting hand. Cup your hand and begin patting baby's back. (See figure 4.1.)

Note: Whenever you pat your baby's back as described here, do so firmly, but avoid using excessive force.

2. Place your baby high on your shoulder with your shoulder placing direct pressure on his or her stomach. The baby's head and arms should freely dangle over your shoulder. Remember to hold on tightly to one leg so your baby doesn't wiggle away from you. Pat the baby's back firmly. (See Figure 4.2.)

3. In a sitting position, place your baby's legs between your legs and drape the baby over your thigh. While supporting the baby's head in your hands, bring your knees together for further support and pat the baby's back firmly. (See Figure 4.3.)

Figure 4.2

4. Cradle the baby in your arm with his or her bottom in your hands. (The baby's head will be resting at your elbow.) Wrap one arm

and leg around your arm. Make sure the baby is facing away from you. This position allows one hand to be free at all times. (See Figure 4.4.)

Note: At times, air will become trapped in the intestines of your baby. Most babies don't like to expel gas. They will tighten their bottoms and resist the normal expulsion of gas, making them very uncomfortable. One way to assist your baby in releasing gas is to place

Figure 4.3

him or her in a knee-chest position. Place your baby's back next to your chest and pull his or her knees up to the chest. This will help to alleviate your baby's discomfort.

Figure 4.4

Questions for Review

1. What is the difference between qualitative and quantitative feedings?

2. What two factors influence breast-milk production? Explain your answer.

3. What are the two sets of response cues? Explain.

4. How long should you nurse your baby the first day, the first week, and after your milk comes in?

5. List two good indicators that your baby is getting enough milk for healthy growth.

    a.

    b.

6. True or False: There is a relationship between the method of infant feeding (breast-feeding versus bottle-feeding) and later personality development.

7. How often should a formula-fed baby be burped?

Chapter Five
....

Monitoring Your Baby's Growth

*I*f you have come this far, chances are you feel convinced. You understand the need for routine feedings within a preset, flexible time frame. You may be willing, if not determined, to breast-feed your baby that most miraculous of foods: mother's milk. Indeed, one of many advantages of parent-directed feeding is the success mothers have with breast-feeding. Knowing her baby's nutritional needs are being met in an orderly fashion gives any woman greater confidence in her role as mother. In addition, establishing a routine gives mother the freedom to maintain relationships outside of motherhood.

So, you have a contented baby and motherhood feels good. You are rested and complete. The confidence is positive but guard against carelessness. Be aware that routine alone won't eliminate every potential lactation problem. Other variables come into play. Factors affecting the routine and attempts to breast-feed include the amount of sleep a mother receives; her diet, nutrition, state of mind, and age; whether this is her first child or her sixth; her desire and physical capacity to breast-feed; her nursing techniques; and the baby's ability to properly latch on.

If you're breast-feeding, monitoring your baby's growth is a vital concern to us and should be to you. Your baby's life depends on it. How do you know if your baby is getting enough food to grow on? There are a number of objective indicators to assist you in the evaluation process. These indicators provide mom with guidance and feedback on how well she and her baby are doing.

As a new mom and dad, knowing what to expect in the first week and having objective markers can make all the difference in the world for your sense of confidence and future direction. At the same time, observing these indicators will help alert you to conditions that may not lead to healthy growth. Poor starts and tragedies can be avoided by monitoring your baby for signs of adequate and inadequate nutrition. If you start to notice the unhealthy indicators, call your pediatrician and report your objective findings.

Included in the back of the book are a series of healthy baby growth charts developed to assist you in your daily evaluation. The first one was designed specifically for your baby's first week of life. The second chart is for weeks two through four, and the third is to be used for weeks five and beyond. Using these charts will provide important benchmarks signaling healthy or unhealthy growth patterns.

What indicators should you look and listen for? Consider the following:

WEEK ONE: Healthy Growth Indicators

1. Under normal circumstances, it takes only a few minutes for your baby to adjust to life outside the womb. His eyes will open and he will begin to seek food. Bring your baby to breast as soon as it is

possible, and certainly try to do so within the first hour and a half after birth. One of the first and most basic positive indicators is your baby's willingness and desire to nurse.

2. It is natural to wonder and to even be a little anxious during the first few postpartum days. How do you know if your baby is getting enough food to live on? The release of the first milk, colostrum, is a second important encouraging indicator. In the simplest terms, colostrum is a protein concentrate ideally suited for your baby's nutritional and health needs.

One of the many benefits of colostrum is its effect on your baby's first bowel movement. It helps trigger the passage of the meconium, your baby's first stools. The meconium stool is greenish black in color with a tarry texture. Newborn stools in the first week transition from meconium to a brownie batter transition stool to a mustard yellow stool. The three to five soft or liquid yellow stools by the fourth or fifth day are totally breast-milk stools and a healthy sign that your baby is getting enough nutrition. A bottle-fed baby will pass firmer, light brown to golden- or clay-colored stools that have an odor similar to adult stools.

3. During this first week, frequent nursing is necessary for two reasons: first, your baby needs the colostrum and second, frequent nursing is required to establish lactation. The fact that your baby nurses every $2^{1}/_2$ to 3 hours and nurses a minimum of eight times a day are two more positive indicators to consider.

4. Just bringing your baby to breast does not mean your baby is nursing efficiently. There is a time element involved. In those early days, most babies nurse between thirty and forty-five minutes. If your baby is sluggish or sleepy all the time or not nursing more than a total

of ten minutes, this may be an unhealthy indicator.

5. As your baby works at taking the colostrum, you will hear him swallow. A typical pattern is suck, suck, suck, then swallow. When mature milk becomes available, your baby responds with a rhythmic suck, swallow, suck, swallow, suck, swallow. You should not hear a clicking sound nor see dimpled cheeks. A clicking sound and dimpled cheeks during nursing are two indicators that your baby is not sucking efficiently. He is sucking his own tongue, not the breast. If you hear clicking, remove baby from the breast and then relatch him. If this continues, contact your pediatrician.

Summary of Week One Growth Indicators

1. Your baby goes to the breast and nurses.

2. Your baby is nursing a minimum of eight times in a twenty-four-hour period.

3. Your baby is nursing over fifteen minutes at each nursing period.

4. You can hear your baby swallowing milk.

5. Your baby has passed his first stool called meconium. (Make sure you let the nurses know that you are tracking your baby's growth indicators.)

6. Your baby's stooling pattern progresses from meconium (greenish black) to brownie batter transition stools to yellow stools by the fourth or fifth day. An increased stooling pattern is one of the most positive signs that your baby is getting enough milk.

7. Within twenty-four to forty-eight hours, your baby starts having wet diapers, (increasing to two or three a day). By the end of the first week wet diapers are becoming more frequent.

Unhealthy Growth Indicators for the First Week

1. Your baby is not showing any desire to nurse or has a very weak suck.

2. Your baby fails to nurse eight times in a twenty-four hour period.

3. Your baby tires quickly at the breast and cannot sustain at least fifteen minutes at the breast.

4. Your baby continually falls asleep at the breast before taking a full feeding.

5. You hear a clicking sound accompanied by dimpled checks while baby is nursing.

6. Your baby's stooling pattern is not progressing to yellow stools within a week's time.

7. Your baby has not wet any diapers within forty-eight hours of birth.

At this point, please turn to the back of the book to look at chart one: review it and remember to bring the book with you to the hospital. If you desire to make additional copies of these charts for your own use, please feel free to do so. (No other part of this book may be reproduced or duplicated in any fashion without written consent of the authors.)

WEEKS TWO THROUGH FOUR: Healthy Growth Indicators

After the first week, some of the healthy growth indicators begin to change. Here is the check list for the next three weeks.

1. Your baby is nursing at least eight times a day.

2. Your baby has two to five or more yellow stools daily during the next three weeks. (This number will probably decrease after the first month.)

3. Your baby during this period should start to have six to eight wet diapers a day (some saturated).

4. Your baby's urine is clear (not yellow).

5. Your baby has a strong suck, you see milk on the corners of his mouth, and you can hear an audible swallow.

6. You're noticing increased signs of alertness during your baby's waketime.

7. Your baby is gaining weight and growing in length. We recommend your baby be weighed within a week or two after birth. Weight gain is one of the surest indicators of growth.

Unhealthy Growth Indicators for Weeks Two through Four

1. Your baby is not getting eight feedings a day.

2. Your baby in the first month has small, scant, and infrequent stools.

3. Your baby does not have the appropriate amount of wet diapers given his age.

4. Your baby's urine is concentrated and bright yellow.

5. Your baby has a weak or nonproductive suck, and you cannot hear him swallow.

6. Your baby is sluggish or slow to respond to stimulus and does not sleep between feedings.

7. Your baby is not gaining weight or growing in length. Your doctor will direct you in the best strategy to correct this problem.

WEEKS FIVE AND ABOVE: Healthy Growth Indicators

The major difference between the first month indicators and the weeks to follow are the stooling patterns. After the first month, your baby's stooling pattern will change. He may pass only one large stool a day or pass one as infrequently as one in every three to five days. Every baby is different. Any concerns regarding elimination should be directed to your pediatrician.

Parents are responsible for seeing that their baby's health and nutritional needs are recognized and met. For your peace of mind and your baby's health, we recommend regular visits with your pediatrician and use of the charts included at the end of the book to monitor and record your baby's progress. Any two consecutive days of deviation from what is listed as normal should be reported to your pediatrician.

If you make copies of the charts, post them in a convenient location such as on the refrigerator, above the crib, or any location that will serve as a convenient reminder. If your baby exhibits any of the unhealthy growth indicators, notify your pediatrician and have your baby weighed.

Weight-Gain Concerns

With the conservative practice of PDF, weight gain will be steady and continuous. We routinely monitor the progress of PDF babies and continue to find wonderful results. In 1997, our retrospective studies tracked and compared the weight gain of 200 *Babywise* infants (group A) and 200 demand-fed infants (group B). Pertinent growth information (weight gain and length) was taken directly from the patient charts of four pediatric practices.

The study's purpose was to determine if faster weight gain can be attributed to a particular method of breast-feeding (routine or demand). The weight and length of each infant was charted at birth,

1 week, 2 weeks, 1, 2, 4, 6, 9 months, and 1 year. Statistical comparisons were made between five weight groups: babies born weighing between 6.50 and 7.0 lbs, 7.1 and 7.50 lbs, 7.51 and 8.0 lbs, 8.1 and 8.50 lbs, and 8.51 and 9.0 lbs. Two methods of analysis were used to compare growth: weight gain ratios (comparing weight gained at each visit as a percentage of birth weight), and Body Mass Index (BMI).[1]

Major Conclusions

1. While there was no significant difference between the two groups, group A (*Babywise* babies) gained weight slightly faster than group B at each weight category.

2. Even when group A began sleeping seven to eight hours at night, there was no significant change in weight-gain performance.

3. While breast-feeding initially was the preferred method for both sets of parents, group B moms gave up breast-feeding significantly sooner than group A.

You can take comfort in the fact that a basic routine will not detract from a proper, healthy weight gain. What it *will* do is facilitate breast-feeding comfort and success. Even low-birthweight babies do well on a conservative routine. Although some newborns start off at the low end of the national norms, they continue to gain weight in proportion to the genetic potential for stature inherited from their parents. That is, smaller parents usually give birth to smaller babies, thus weight gain will usually be proportionately less. Add to these weight-gain benefits for baby the pleasure of a solid night's sleep for both parents, and the greater benefits of PDF become obvious. If you have a low-weight-gain baby, seek your physician's specific recommendations as to how often your baby should be fed.

Normal Weight-Gain Guide

Birth to Two Weeks:

Approximate average: Regain birth weight plus.

Two Weeks to Three Months:

Approximate average: Two pounds per month or one ounce per day.

Four to Six Months:

Approximate average: One pound per month or one-half ounce per day. (Doubles his or her birth weight by six months.)

One Year:

Approximate average: Two and a half to three times his or her birth weight.

Babies Who Fail to Thrive

There is a difference between *slow weight gain* and *failure to thrive*. With slow weight gain, weight gain is slow but consistent. Failure to thrive describes an infant who continues to lose weight after ten days of life, does not regain his or her birth weight by three weeks of age, or gains at an unusually slow rate beyond the first month. It's estimated that in the United States, more than two hundred thousand babies a year experience failure to thrive. The cause can be attributed to either mother or child.

Mother-Related Causes

Here are some matters specific to mother that can contribute to slow or no weight gain.

1. *Improper nursing technique.* Many women fail at breast-feeding because the baby is not positioned properly on the breast. As a result, he or she latches on only to the nipple and not to all or much of the areola. The end result is a hungry baby.

2. *Nature or lifestyle.* Insufficient milk production can be a result of nature (insufficient glandular tissue or hormones) or a mother's lifestyle (not getting enough rest or liquids). The mother simply doesn't produce enough milk, or in some cases, milk of high enough quality. If you suspect this is the case, try a) using a breast pump to see what quantity of milk is being produced and b) discovering if your baby will take any formula after he or she has been at your breast for the proper amount of time. Report your findings to your pediatrician.

3. *Poor release of milk.* This indicates a problem with the mother's let-down reflex.

4. *Feeding too frequently.* There is an irony here because one would think that many feedings ensure adequate weight gain. Not necessarily! In some cases a mother can be worn out by too many ineffective feedings. When we first met Jeffrey, he was six weeks old and had gained only one pound. His mom offered him the breast each time he cried, approximately every 1 to 1½ hours. Jeffrey was properly latched on to his fatigued and frustrated mother.

Although he was failing to thrive, the only counsel this mother received was to feed more often. To further her exhaustion, she was told to constantly carry Jeffrey in a sling. Immediately, we put Jeffrey's mother on a three-hour routine. To improve Jeffrey's poor health, he was given a formula supplement. Within a few days, the starving child started to gain weight. After just a week, he was sleeping through the night. Jeffrey's mother successfully breast-fed his subsequent siblings on the PDF plan with no weight-gain problems.

5. *Feeding too infrequently.* This problem can be attributed to either hyperscheduling or demand-feeding. The mother who insists on watching the clock to the minute lacks confidence in decision-making. The clock is in control, not the parent. The hyperschedulist insists on a strict schedule, often nursing her baby no more often than every four hours. Enslavement to the clock is almost as great an evil as a mother who is in bondage to thoughtless emotions.

Another side to the problem of infrequency is that some demand-fed babies demand too little food. As a result, the mother's breast is not sufficiently stimulated for adequate milk production. Routine feedings with a time limitation between feedings eliminates this problem. That's why neonatal and intensive care units stay close to a three-hour feeding schedule. It's healthy.

6. *Not monitoring growth signs.* Many moms simply fail to notice their baby's healthy and unhealthy growth indicators. The healthy baby growth chart will assist you with this vital task.

7. *Physical nurturing, holding, and cuddling.* The lack of these gestures can impact a child's ability to thrive. It is important that moms cuddle, hold, and talk to their babies frequently throughout the day. Your routine will help provide these periods, but mom should not be the only one cuddling the child. Dad, older siblings, grandma, and

grandpa are some of your baby's favorite people. More people, more love.

Infant-Related Causes

Slow weight gain or an absence of weight gain also may be directly related to your infant. Here are several possibilities.

1. *Weak sucking.* In this case, the child doesn't have the coordination or the strength to suck properly, remain latched on, or activate the let-down reflex. As a result, the baby receives the low-calorie foremilk but not the high-calorie hindmilk.

2. *Improper sucking.* This can result from a number of different conditions:

   a. Tongue thrusting. When going to breast, sometimes a baby thrusts his or her tongue forward and pushes the nipple out of his or her mouth.
   b. Protruding tongue. This condition is described as the tongue forming a hump in the mouth, interfering with successful latching on.
   c. Tongue sucking. The infant suckles on his own tongue.

3. *An underlying medical problem.* A weak or laborious suck (for example, one in which the child tires to the point of giving up after a few minutes of nursing) can be a symptom of cardiac or neurological failing. If you suspect this may be the case, don't wait for your baby's next scheduled checkup. Call your pediatrician immediately. There are many variables involved in successful breast-milk production and fortunately, your baby's routine is a healthy one.

Getting the Necessary Help

Contacting a Lactation Consultant

Even with all the classes we take, the plans we make and books we read, sometimes nursing just doesn't go well. It can be very frustrating in those first few days or weeks. There you are, holding a crying, wiggling, red-faced (but cute) little bundle who can't or won't nurse, and all your interventions seem of no avail.

You may need help from a lactation consultant. These are professionals skilled in identifying and correcting lactation difficulties. Your pediatrician's office, hospital, or clinic will often have a consultant on staff or can refer you to one. We highly recommend you choose one who is licensed and board certified. Be aware that those who practice independently tend to have higher fees than those who are affiliated with a medical practice. Check with your insurance company to find out if the cost is covered under your plan.

If you can, schedule your initial visit near a feeding time. Your consultant usually will want to observe the baby nursing. She will also weigh the infant and check to see that his suckle is correct. Next, a history will be taken, including questions about the length of labor, birth, birth weight of the baby, your diet, how often you are nursing the baby, and more. The information logged on your healthy baby growth chart is useful to the consultant. It provides an overall picture of how your infant is doing. Certain conditions like inverted or flat nipples, which can make nursing difficult, may be modified or corrected prenatally. If this is your situation, you might benefit by making an appointment with a consultant early in your third trimester.

Unfortunately, as a result of their training many within the lactation industry are heavily biased in favor of the attachment parenting theories and thus against any type of routine feeding. PDF is a new and major paradigm shift for the industry and not all consultants have a working understanding of routine breast-feeding dynamics. While many consultants are open and sensitive to you as consumer and want to work with you as a mother and help facilitate your goals, others unfortunately are less receptive to your efforts. As a result, do not be surprised if the concept of putting a nursing infant on a "flexible routine" is questioned.

Openly share actual feeding times and precisely what you are doing. Cite all the sources for feeding time recommendations found in chapter four. Although parenting philosophies will differ, any technical lactation intervention is applicable, whether you demand-feed or use a routine. If you hear something that does not sound right or seems extreme, consider getting a second opinion, keeping in mind what is normal for attachment-parenting babies is not necessarily normal for PDF babies. Likewise, if you are told to feed your baby every hour and a half, carry him in a sling, and sleep with him, consider looking elsewhere for a solution.

In some cases, intervention and correction are immediate. In others, such as with those infants who have a disorganized or a dysfunctional suckle, retraining the infant to suckle correctly will take some time and patience on your part. Depending on the circumstance, the lactation consultant might suggest using devices such as a syringe (minus the needle), finger-feeding, or a supplemental feeding device to help your infant learn to nurse. Sometimes these are effective, other times they are not. They also can be time consuming to use. Discuss the choices with your husband and make your decision together. Should you use a device, reevaluate its effectiveness at some point.

Breast-feeding proficiency is usually a matter of standard review in childbirth classes. For additional help, consider taking a breast-feeding class at your local hospital or renting a how-to video. You can attend a class and learn proper techniques of breast-feeding without accepting the instructor's personal parenting philosophies that sometimes accompany such classes. Remember to keep the issue of nursing in balance. Going the "extra mile" to correct a nursing difficulty or deciding to stop and bottle-feed instead is not a positive or negative reflection on your mothering. What is important is that your husband and you decide what is best for your baby.

Insufficient Milk Production

Regardless of which feeding philosophy you follow, you cannot add to what nature has left out. The anxiety created by the fear of failure is itself a contributor to milk deficiency. Because so much guilt is placed on mothers who are not successful at breast-feeding, many of them go to extremes to become milk-sufficient.

In most cultures, 5 percent of nursing mothers during peacetime and up to 10 percent during wartime will not produce enough milk to satisfy their infants' needs. Some mothers may initially be milk-sufficient but become insufficient by the third month. This sometimes happens even though baby is cooperative and sucking frequently and mom is using correct nursing techniques, receiving adequate food and rest, and has sufficient support from her husband and family.

If You Question Your Milk Supply

If at any time you question the adequacy of your milk supply, observe routine fussiness after every feeding, or your baby is having difficulty going the appropriate duration between feedings, review the external stresses in your life. Eliminate what you can. This is true whether baby is four weeks old or four months old.

Ask yourself the following: Are you too busy or not getting enough sleep? Are you drinking enough liquids? Is your intake of calories adequate? Are you dieting too soon, or are you on birth control pills? Are you following your doctor's recommendation for supplemental vitamins during lactation? Also consider the technical aspects associated with feeding. Is the baby positioned properly and latched on correctly? Is your baby taking a full feeding from both breasts?

1. If you question your milk supply in the first two months: for a baby between three and eight weeks old, consider feeding on a strict 2¹/₂-hour routine for five to seven days. If your milk production increases (as demonstrated by the baby becoming more content and sleeping better), work your way back to the three hour minimum. If no improvement comes, work back up to three hours with the aid of a formula complement for the benefit of your baby and your own peace of mind.

2. If you question your milk supply in the fourth month: the same basic principles apply to this age category. If your baby is between four and six months of age and you question your milk supply, try adding a couple of feedings to your daytime routine. One of our mothers, also a pediatrician, felt she was losing her milk supply at four months. She did two things. She added a fifth feeding to her day,

and she stopped dieting. In less than one week her milk supply was back to normal.

Other mothers find success by returning to a fairly tight three-hour schedule. Once their milk supply returns to normal, they gradually return to their previous routine. If no improvement comes after five to seven days, consider a formula complement. Adding a few extra feedings during the day is not a setback in your parenting but necessary to insure a healthy balance between breast-feeding and the related benefits of PDF.

The Four Day Test

You may also want to consider the four day test. This involves offering a complementary feeding of one to two ounces of formula after each nursing period. Then, express your milk with an electric breast pump ten minutes per side. (Manual pumps are not effective for this purpose.) Keep track of how much extra you are producing. If your milk is plentiful, then the problem lies with your baby. He or she is either not latching on properly or is a lazy nurser. If your milk supply increases as a result of pumping, which will be indicated either by milk expressed or by your baby not wanting the complementary feeding, then return to breast-feeding only, maintaining a three-hour routine.

If additional stimulation from breast pumping doesn't increase your milk supply, and if you have reviewed all the external factors and found them compatible with nursing, then you may be among the 5 percent of moms who can't provide a sufficient milk supply. Are you ready to give it up? Before you say "that's me" and quit for good, consider calling your pediatrician for advice. Ask if he or she knows of an older mother in the practice who was able to reverse this situation. You may also be referred to a lactation consultant. One final caution: avoid extreme recommendations that can worsen your condition. Remember, different opinions abound. Learn and discern what is best for your family. Then make a commitment with no excuses needed.

Questions for Review

1. List some variables influencing your routine and desire to breast-feed.

2. What is the healthy baby growth chart? What purpose does it serve?

3. Describe the difference between slow weight gain and failure-to-thrive babies.

4. What is a symptom of an underlying medical problem in a baby? Describe the condition.

5. What should you do if by the end of the third week your baby is not going $2^{1}/_{2}$ to 3 hours on mother's milk?

....

Chapter Six

Establishing Your Baby's Routine

*D*ay one. There's no better time to begin thinking about your baby's routine. While all the pieces may not fall into place for another three or four days, you should still be thinking about your long-term strategy now. Whether you have just one baby or a whole bushel, consistency of care will establish peace for all. At the heart of this plan lie three basic activities. Baby is fed. Baby is awake. Baby sleeps. With the exception of the late-night and the middle-of-the-night feedings when waketime is not necessary, this order should not be altered.

For the first week, consistently achieving this sequence with your newborn may seem an insurmountable task. Let's face it. Newborns are sleepyheads. You may find that after many of your feedings baby drifts determinedly back to sleep. Attempts to keep awake this sweet bundle simply are not successful. This is okay. Wakefulness is a goal to strive toward. Exercise the effort now toward giving full feedings and by week two your baby most likely will fall into a predictable feed/wake/sleep routine. When this happens, you are off and running. With parent-directed feeding, your baby wins the ribbon of confidence knowing you indeed are in control.

How you first meet your baby's feeding and nutritional needs says a world about your overall parenting philosophy. These moments of nurturing do far more than fill a little belly. With feeding, you are integrating life into your child and your child into life. Shouldn't so significant a process require a fully developed plan? Whether nourishment is provided by breast or by bottle, the guidelines which follow will assist in your success.

Your Lifestyle and Your Baby

Rod and Colleen are a disciplined couple. They are neat, orderly, precise, and systematic in everything they do. There is a place for everything, and everything is in its place. This couple would never dream of leaving a pair of muddy loafers at the back door. Early risers, they have jogged two miles, showered, and are prepared to sit down for breakfast—all by 6:30 A.M. Dinner typically is served at the same time each evening, and the activities of the day are fairly predictable. Their lifestyle represents a tight routine.

If you feel Rod and Colleen have life just a bit too together, maybe you lean more towards the lifestyle of Dave and Kim. This couple seems comfortable with a little more flex in their lives. They appreciate things which are neat and orderly, precise and systematic, but consider some types of confusion to be an art form. If the day doesn't turn out as planned, no big deal. Sometimes they rise at 6:30 A.M. while other days they sleep longer. Perhaps they even daydream about an entire Saturday spent lounging in bed. Mealtimes are anything but rigid, easily worked in around the day's activities. This lifestyle represents a loose routine.

Look at your spouse and you as a couple. Which of the two personal styles named above best represents your duo? Is life very predictable, or are you comfortable with variations in routine? If you view life most like Rod and Colleen, you will have a tendency to establish a tighter routine for baby. In contrast, being a couple more like Dave and Kim means feeding periods will have some flex to them. For example, some days Kim's baby will receive his first feeding at 6:30 A.M. Other days it may be 7:00 A.M. before baby gets food. When this happens, Kim automatically adjusts the baby's morning routine based on this feeding. Regardless of parenting style, your baby soon learns to fit with your personal style.

Flexibility

Whether you are a Rod and Colleen, a Dave and Kim, or any combination in between, flexibility is basic to your success. But what is flexibility? Many times we hear new moms say they want to be flexible. What does this look like? The word flexibility means the ability to bend or be pliable. When you think of a flexible item, you think of something with a particular shape that can bend and then return to its original shape. Returning is perhaps the most crucial element of flexing. During the critical first weeks of stabilization, you are giving your baby's routine its shape. Too much "flexibility" in these weeks is viewed by a baby as inconsistency.

Routine must first be established. After that, when necessary deviations are made, baby will bounce back to the original routine. Doing so, however, may require your firm guidance. The flexibility you desire will come, but give yourself time to develop your child's routine. And remember, true flexibility is not a lack of routine, but a temporary alteration of what you normally do.

Your Baby's First Year

Your baby's first year is divided into four basic phases.

Phase 1:   Stabilization. Birth through week eight.
Phase 2:   Extended Night. Weeks nine through fifteen.
Phase 3:   Extended Day. Weeks sixteen through twenty-four.
Phase 4:   Extended Routine. Weeks twenty-four through fifty-two.

In this chapter, our focus is confined to feeding times and activities related to feeding. In the next chapter, we will focus on wake-time activities and naptime.

Phase One: Stabilization
Birth through Eight Weeks

During the first four or five days, a daily routine for most new mothers will be a continual repeat of a 2½- to 3-hour cycle from the beginning of one feeding to the beginning of the next. Feeding times and sleep times initially will be more constant than waketimes. That again is due to the natural sleepiness of your baby in the early postpartum days. By the end of the first week, waketimes will start to become predictable and constant.

Both baby and mom need to achieve a few basic goals during this phase. For the breast-feeding mother, the establishment of stable milk production is the main objective. For baby, the stabilization of hunger metabolism as well as stabilized sleep/wake cycles are primary goals. Possibly an additional goal may be teaching your baby how to nurse.

One caution for new parents is to stay mindful of your newborn's sleepiness. A newborn tends to fall asleep at the breast before he is done nursing. Baby only wants to snack. The parents must keep him awake until a full feeding is over. Rub his toes, change his diaper, share your deepest thoughts. Baby is a good listener and will enjoy the sound of your voice. Truly strive to keep him awake until after the feeding period is completed. Remember, exerting the extra energy will pay off soon enough. Plus, it's a health issue. Babies who love snacking at the breast too often fail to get crucial hindmilk rich in calories.

General Guidelines

Don't underestimate the following six guidelines. Although simple, they will bring order to your life and make you a confident, more competent parent.

1. Understand how to calculate time between feedings. As previously mentioned in chapter 4, the time between feedings should be measured from the beginning of one feeding to the beginning of the next. In every feeding cycle, plan approximately 1/2 hour for feeding. For example, two-week-old Chelsea was on a 3-hour routine. She

received a feeding at 7:00 A.M. Her mom nursed her for 30 minutes—7:30 A.M. If Chelsea receives her next feeding in 2$1/2$ hours, at 10:00 A.M., then 3 hours will have elapsed from the start of one feeding to the start of the next. Keep in mind that the clock is only your guide. If your baby shows signs of hunger before her next scheduled feeding time—feed her.

2. Between weeks one and four, nurse your baby every 2$1/2$ to 3 hours. Any combination with these time frames is acceptable. During these early weeks stay close to these recommended times. These routine feedings will help to establish and stabilize both your lactation and your baby's metabolism. You want to average 8 to 10 feedings in a 24-hour period.

NOTE: If you need to awaken your baby during the day to prevent him or her from sleeping longer than the 3-hour cycle, do so! Such parental intervention is necessary to help stabilize the baby's digestive metabolism, and it helps him to organize his sleep. If you find that your baby just won't wake up enough to feed, than give him an extra 30 minutes sleep and try again. The exception to this guideline comes with the late-evening feedings. After the late-evening feeding, usually 10:00 or 11:00 P.M., let the baby sleep as long as he will, but never more than five hours if you are breast-feeding. When he does wake, feed him and put him right back to bed.

3. After the first week, starting with the early-morning feeding and continuing through the mid-evening feeding, all three activities will take place: feeding time, waketime, and naptime. During the late evening and nighttime segment, there should be no extended wake periods. Feed your baby and put him or her right back to bed.

4. Between weeks five and eight, starting with your early-morning

feeding and continuing through the mid-evening feeding, you will feed your baby between 2^1/2 and 3^1/2 hours. Any time increment between those two times is acceptable. Even with an increase in time flexibility, plan an average of eight feedings a day. Understand that some babies may need to feed more often, others less. One question commonly asked is this: "At this age, my baby is doing well with only seven nursing periods a day. Should I try to force an eighth feeding?" Some babies do well with seven feedings by this age. Remember, the premise of PDF is that you, the parent, are directing feedings based on your assessment of your baby's needs. Regardless of what number is right for your baby, stay mindful of all healthy baby indicators.

5. When you establish your baby's routine, first consider all your activities such as grocery shopping, work, exercise, household chores, and church attendance. There will be times when your baby's routine will change to fit into your schedule. Other times, you will plan your activity around your baby's needs, simply because it is more practical to do so. With a routine you have this type of flexibility. Without a routine, you are subject to the irregular needs of the child.

6. Determine the time of your day's first feeding. This time will be fairly consistent each day and may be initially set by both your baby and you. Make certain you establish one. This, too, will help organize your baby's feed/wake/sleep cycles.

Summary of Phase One

By the end of eight weeks, the stabilization phase is usually complete. By this time, your baby should be sleeping through the night on a regular basis or very close to achieving the skill. If she is not, don't worry. Approximately 15 percent of PDF babies will start sleeping through the night between weeks ten and twelve. At this point, they catch right up to all the other PDF babies.

The number of feedings in a 24-hour period will be seven to nine before your baby is sleeping through the night, and seven to eight feedings afterwards. Although you will be dropping the nighttime feeding at this point, you will not be reducing your baby's caloric intake, just rearranging feeding times. Babies tend to compensate for the one lost nighttime feeding by consuming more milk during other periods.[1]

You may need to maintain a seventh or eighth feeding period for four to five days after your baby initially begins sleeping through the night. Sticking close to a $2^1/2$- to 3-hour routine will help facilitate that goal. Some mothers find those times more in line with their comfort zone and stay there several weeks. Most PDF moms are comfortable alternating between a $2^1/2$- and $3^1/2$-hour routine, getting in six good nursing periods.

Feeding at Intervals Less Than $2^1/2$ Hours

As stated, your baby's normal feeding periods fall between $2^1/2$- and 3-hour intervals. But there are times when you may feed sooner than those time increments. For example, the late afternoon for many nursing mothers is usually when their milk supply is at its lowest point quantitatively and qualitatively. This is usually due to mother's busy day. As a result, there may be an early-evening feeding as soon as two hours after the last feeding.

There may be medical reasons for feeding a child more frequently. For example, some premature newborns or very small full-term infants, such as those with intrauterine growth retardation, may need to feed as often as every two hours initially. In addition, if your child has jaundice and requires the use of phototherapy lights, he will lose more fluids from exposure. Therefore he may need to feed more frequently. Your doctor will direct you in this area.

Your late-evening feeding, falling somewhere between 8:30 P.M. and midnight, is another example of when you might drop below the 2 1/2-hour mark. Some mothers feed their babies at 8:30 P.M. and then again at 10:30 P.M. Here the decision to feed within two hours is a practical one. Now both mom and baby can go to bed earlier. The point is this: it's okay to deviate from the 2 1/2- to 3-hour feeding norm. But do not deviate so often that you establish a new norm.

What should you do if your baby sleeps through the night only to awaken at 5:00 A.M. when his normal routine does not officially start until 6:30 A.M.? You have three choices. First, you may wait ten to fifteen minutes to make sure he is truly awake. He may be passing through an active sleep state, moving to deeper sleep. Second, you can feed your baby and then put him back down. You can then awaken him at 7:00 A.M. and feed him again. Although that is less than three hours and he may not take much at that feeding, the advantage will be that your baby stays on his morning routine. A third option is to offer a feeding at 5:00 A.M., treating that as your first feeding of the day. In that case, you would adjust the rest of the baby's morning schedule so that by early afternoon he is back on his daily routine.

Considering Context and Being Flexible

Earlier we talked about being flexible. What does it look like and how do you know what circumstances call for flexibility? Most notable in a person who lacks flexibility is his or her rejection of context. Responding to the context of a situation does not mean suspending the principles of PDF. Rather, you are able to focus on the right response in the short term without compromising your long-term objectives. As stated above, there will be times when a situation dictates a temporary suspension of the guidelines presented. Remember you are the parent—endowed with experience, wisdom, and common sense. Trust these attributes first, not an extreme of emotion or the rigidity of the clock. When special situations arise, allow context to be your guide.

Here are some examples of context and PDF flexibility:

1. Your two-week-old baby boy was sleeping contentedly until his older brother decided to make a social call. Big brother notifies you that baby is awake and crying. Another thirty minutes are left before his next scheduled feeding. What should you do? First, you can try settling the baby back down by patting him on the back or holding him. Placing him in his infant seat is a second option. A third option is to feed him and rework the next feed/wake/nap cycle. (Also, instruct the older brother to check with you before he visits his sleeping sibling.)

2. You are on an airplane and your infant daughter begins to fuss. The fussing grows louder. You fed her just two hours earlier. Yet failure to act will stress you, not to mention the entire jet full of people. What should you do? Your solution is simple: consider others. Don't let your baby's routine get in the way of being thoughtful toward others. You can either attempt to play with your baby and entertain her or you can feed her. Although you normally would not offer food before three hours have passed from your last feeding, the context of the situation dictates that you suspend your normal routine. When you arrive at your destination, you can get back to basics. There's your flex!

3. You have been driving for four hours, which is your baby son's normal time between feedings. Your baby is still asleep and you have another forty minutes to travel. As a parent in control, you may choose to awaken your baby and feed him (pull over first!) or wait until you get to your destination.

4. You just fed your baby daughter and dropped her off at the church nursery or with your baby-sitter. You are planning to return within an hour and a half. Should you leave a bottle of breast milk or formula just in case? Most certainly, yes. Baby-sitters and nursery workers provide a valuable service to young parents. Because their care extends to other children, they should not be obligated to follow your routine exactly as you do. If your baby fusses, you will want the caretaker to have the option of offering a bottle (even though it will have been less than three hours). It won't throw your child off her routine to receive early feedings a few times each week.

Most of your day will be fairly routine and predictable. But there will be times when you may need more flexibility due to unusual circumstances. Your life will be less tense if you consider the context of each situation and respond appropriately for the benefit of everyone. Right parental responses often determine whether a child is a blessing to others or a source of discomfort.

Sample Schedule

Below, we have provided a sample schedule which can be personalized for you and your baby. Remember the basic rule: feed every $2^1/2$ to 3 hours after the beginning of the last feeding. Then baby needs waketime, which is followed by naptime. The various activities listed alongside the waketimes are suggestions. This work sheet is based on eight feedings in a 24-hour period and is a guide for your first six to eight weeks.

FEEDING	WHAT TO DO
Early Morning _____ A.M.	1. Feeding and diaper change. 2. Waketime: Rock your baby and sing; place your baby on his or her back in the crib to watch a mobile. 3. Put your baby down for a nap.
Midmorning _____ A.M.	1. Feeding and diaper change. 2. Waketime: Take a walk with your baby, run errands or visit neighbors. 3. Put your baby down for a nap.
Afternoon _____ P.M.	1. Feeding and diaper change. 2. Waketime: Bathe your baby and place him or her in an infant seat near a window. 3. Put your baby down for a nap.
Midafternoon _____ P.M.	1. Feeding and diaper change. 2. Waketime: Play with your baby; have him or her by your side as you read or sew. 3. Put your baby down for a nap.

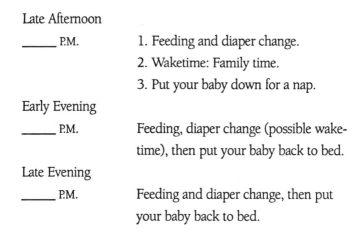

Late Afternoon

_____ P.M.
1. Feeding and diaper change.
2. Waketime: Family time.
3. Put your baby down for a nap.

Early Evening

_____ P.M.
Feeding, diaper change (possible waketime), then put your baby back to bed.

Late Evening

_____ P.M.
Feeding and diaper change, then put your baby back to bed.

NOTE: For many babies, this feeding is the last scheduled feeding of the day. If this is the case with your baby, do not wake him for his next feeding. Let him wake up naturally. If breast-feeding, however, do not let him go longer than five hours at night for the first four weeks.

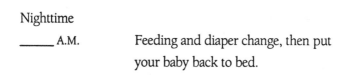

Nighttime

_____ A.M.
Feeding and diaper change, then put your baby back to bed.

When a breast-fed baby initially begins sleeping through the night, mom may experience some slight discomfort for the first couple of mornings. For some of these moms, it may take a couple of days for their bodies to make the proper adjustments to the longer nighttime sleep. If you feel uncomfortable after the first morning feeding, pump until you are comfortable. This will be temporary. Within a week's time both mom and baby should have adjusted to their new sleep/wake patterns.

Phase Two: Extended Night

Weeks Nine through Fifteen

During this second phase, a breast-fed baby can gradually extend his nighttime sleep to nine to ten hours, and a bottle-fed baby can go eleven hours. Make a note that breast-feeding mothers must stay mindful of their milk production. Letting your baby sleep longer than nine or ten hours at night may not afford you enough time during the day for sufficient stimulation. That is not true for all mothers, but it is for some. Therefore, if you are breast-feeding and are concerned about a decrease in your milk supply, we recommend that you do not let your baby sleep longer than ten hours at night during this phase.

Bedtime during this phase will be adjusted closer to the early-evening feeding. By the end of the thirteenth week, your baby should average five to six feedings a day, but never less than four.

Phase Three: Extended Day

Weeks Sixteen through Twenty-four

Usually between the sixteenth and twenty-fourth week, you will introduce your baby to solid foods. Your pediatrician will direct you in that area. Along with solid foods, continue with four to six liquid feedings. During phase three, most babies are sleeping ten to eleven hours at night. Again, breast-feeding mothers must continually monitor their milk supply. If you feel you need to add an additional feeding during the day, do it.

By the twenty-fourth week your baby's mealtimes should begin to line up with the rest of the family's: breakfast, lunch, and dinner, with a fourth, fifth, and for some, a sixth liquid feeding at bedtime. As you begin introducing solids to your baby's diet, please note that you are not adding more feeding periods, just additional food at breakfast, lunch, and dinner. If you are breast-feeding, nurse first and then offer some cereal. If you are bottle-feeding, offer some formula, then offer cereal, followed by formula. Do not offer cereal alone with a supplemental liquid feeding two hours later. That would mean you are feeding every two hours, which is not a healthy habit. Introducing solid foods is a topic discussed in detail in *On Becoming Babywise II: Parenting Your Pretoddler.* As a breast-feeding mother, try to maintain four to six feeding periods as long as you are nursing. Any less may decrease your milk supply.

Phase Four: Extended Routine

Weeks Twenty-five through Fifty-two

Between the ages of six months and twelve months, your baby will continue to be fed on three meals a day. Each meal is supplemented by baby food with an optional fourth liquid feeding before bed. At this age your baby should be taking two naps averaging from $1^{1}/_{2}$ to $2^{1}/_{2}$ hours in length. Continue with four to five nursing periods during the day. This same general rule applies to formula-fed babies (see chapter 4, "Facts on Feeding").

Summary of First-Year Feeding

For easy reference, the following summary of your baby's first year of feeding is provided.

Phase One: Weeks One through Eight

Start with eight or more feedings for the first two to three weeks. After that you may average eight feedings over the course of the next six weeks. The number of feedings will depend on whether you begin with a flexible 2½- to 3-hour routine or strict 2½- or 3-hour routine. By the end of this phase, you should be averaging seven to eight feedings in a 24-hour period and most likely will not have a middle-of-the-night feeding.

Phase Two: Weeks Nine through Fifteen

From the beginning of this phase until the end of it, most PDF moms transition from seven or eight feedings down to five to seven feedings in a 24-hour period. (Please note these are averages—not absolutes.) Between weeks twelve and fifteen, most babies go easily to a combination 3- to 4-hour routine and drop the late-evening feeding.

Phase Three: Weeks Sixteen through Twenty-four

Your baby will maintain four to six liquid feedings in a 24-hour period, three of which will be supplemented with baby food.

Phase Four: Weeks Twenty-five through Fifty-two

The process of moving a child to three meals a day should be nearly completed by the beginning of this phase. Remember that at each meal there needs to be a time of nursing, plus a fourth nursing period just before bed.

How to Drop a Feeding

By dropping a feeding, we don't mean your baby will take in less food over a 24-hour period. Actually, the amount will gradually increase although the frequency of feedings will decrease. As your baby begins to take in more food at each feeding and his metabolism stabilizes, you will begin dropping a feeding period. The three most common ways to do this follow:

1. Change from a 3-hour to a 3$^{1}/_{2}$-hour schedule, or from a 3$^{1}/_{2}$-hour to a 4-hour schedule. If you have to consistently wake your baby for his or her daytime feedings, this is a strong indication that the baby can go longer between feedings. Generally, your baby will be capable of moving to a flexible 3- to 4-hour routine by three months of age.

2. Drop the middle-of-the-night feeding. Many babies drop this feeding on their own between the seventh and ninth week. One night they simply sleep until morning. Some babies gradually stretch the distance between the 10:00 P.M. and the 6:00 A.M. feedings.

There are some little ones whose internal clocks get "stuck" at the nighttime feeding. Parental guidance can help reset that clock. If you have a digital timepiece and notice that your baby is waking at nearly the same time each night, that's a strong indicator that his or her biological clock is stuck. To correct the problem, wait for a weekend when no one has to get up early for work. (You may want to sleep in if your sleep is disturbed by your baby's crying during the night.) When your baby awakens, don't rush right in to him or her. Any crying will be temporary, lasting from five to forty-five minutes. Remember, this will be temporary! Some parents fear that failing to respond right away will make their baby feel unloved or insecure. On the contrary, it's cruel not to help your child gain the skill of sleeping through the night. Taking the baby into bed with you will delay the learning process. Generally, it takes three nights to establish a new routine that allows for continuous sleep for both mom and baby.

3. Drop the late-evening feeding. This process occurs anywhere from two months of age on and is usually the trickiest feeding to eliminate. Having grown accustomed to sleeping all night, some parents are reluctant to drop the late-evening feeding for fear that the baby will awaken in the middle of the night, starving.

Sometimes in the process of eliminating feedings, bending a guideline may be necessary. If we assume your baby is on a 4-hour schedule (6:00 A.M., 10:00 A.M., 2:00 P.M., 6:00 P.M., and 10:00 P.M.), and you think he or she is ready to drop the last feeding, then instead of eliminating the 10:00 P.M. feeding completely, try backing it up fifteen minutes per day until you arrive at the time you desire. For a while, your baby's last two feedings of the day may be less than three hours apart, which is permissible during this transition time. The rest of the day's schedule may need to be adjusted so that you end up with a new 4-hour format which looks like this: feedings at 8:00 A.M., 12:00 P.M., 4:00 P.M., and 8:00 P.M. (or whatever times best suit your family).

Questions for Review

1. List the three activities of your baby's routine.

    a.

    b.

    c.

2. From the list above, what exception applies to the late-evening and middle-of-the-night feedings?

3. How do you measure the time between feedings?

4. When should you wake a sleeping baby, and when should you let him sleep?

5. Give some examples of when you would feed sooner than 2^1/$_2$ hours.

6. How long can you let a breast-fed baby sleep at night during phase two, nine to fifteen weeks? Explain your answer.

7. Responding to context helps you to do what?

Chapter Seven

Waketime and Naptime

*I*n this chapter we will examine the last two activities in your baby's routine: waketime and naptime. Much of what is discussed in this chapter deals specifically with a child who is at least one week old. That statement is not to suggest that parental guidance is not necessary in the first week, but that a baby is better able to respond to your leadership starting in week two when life begins to settle in for both of you.

One of the most common mistakes made when following a routine is to reverse the order of these last two activities—that is, putting the baby down for a nap right after his or her feeding. This will be one of your greatest challenges during the first week. Babies are usually sleepy during the first several days, causing some to fall asleep right at the breast after a few minutes of nursing. That means you have to work on keeping your baby awake to take a full feeding. (Rub his feet, stroke his face, change a diaper, talk to him, remove his sleeper, but he must eat.) Snacking five minutes every hour is not a full feeding. Mothers who work to get a full feeding during the first week have a baby who naturally transitions into a consistent three-hour routine within seven to ten days. Keep this goal in mind when putting in the extra effort. The payoff comes in confidence and comfort for both baby and you.

Even with all this encouragement, there may be a meal or two when your baby will not wake up sufficiently to take a full feeding. What will you do in those times? If your attempts to keep him awake fail, put your baby down to sleep but work on feeding him again in an hour or two, or anytime your baby signals hunger readiness. The newness of parenting can bring about some anxious moments, especially if you have a sleepyhead on your hands. But rest assured, in a few days life will become more predictable for you and your baby, and your planned pattern of routine feedings with your baby completely participating will begin to take shape.

Waketime activities include times when you and your baby will be together and times when your baby will explore his or her new world alone.

Mom, Dad, and Baby Together

Feeding: Whether bottle- or breast-feeding, you will spend much of your day holding your baby while feeding him or her.

Singing: At birth, a baby responds to his or her mom and dad's voices. Talk and sing to your baby during waketimes, remembering that learning is always taking place.

Reading: It's never too soon to read to your baby or to show the baby colorful picture books (especially cardboard or plastic ones that the baby can explore on his or her own). Your infant loves to hear the sound of your voice and inflections.

Bathing: This is another pleasant routine for you and your baby. You can sing, tell your child which part of his or her body you are washing, or just have fun splashing.

Walking: Taking time for a stroll outside is great for you and your little one. You can sing or talk while you are walking, and the fresh air is good for both of you.

Playing: Initially, you can't play much with a newborn. A few early play activities are flirting with your baby, smiling, talking, and gently moving his or her arms and legs and, of course, cuddling with your newborn. That is more than fun; it is a necessary way to express physical love to him or her.

Baby Alone

Pictures: Putting bright pictures and patterns around the nursery is a great way to stimulate your baby visually.

Mobiles: Moving, musical mobiles help your baby learn to track with his or her eyes.

Gym: Crib gyms and objects that dangle over your baby and rattle when he or she bats at them help to develop her hand-eye coordination. Batting is the necessary preparation for reaching out and holding objects. (For safety's sake, the crib gym should not be dangled over the baby once the child learns to sit up.)

Swing: Putting a baby in a swing allows your infant to watch what is going on around him or her. Swings are especially helpful for calming fussy newborns. However, don't get into the habit of letting your baby fall asleep in a swing, since the child needs to learn to fall asleep without this prop.

Infant Seat: This item provides another way you can help your baby to sit up and take notice of the world. Sometimes toys or books can be hung from an overhead handle.

Playpen: Start at one month of age with the playpen. A four-week-old baby can spend some waketime in an infant seat placed inside the playpen in view of a mobile. Also, allow the child to take a nap in the playpen once in a while.

Having some of this equipment—whether new, used, or borrowed—is helpful, but it is certainly not a necessity. In addition to feeding, changing, and bathing your baby, you might have at least one playtime a day when the baby has your full attention for fifteen minutes or so. Dad also needs to spend time each day with the baby in addition to possible feeding times.

Naptime

Naps are not an option based on your baby's wants. When naptime comes, the baby goes down. It is that simple. For optimal development, infants need daytime rest. In following your feeding, wake, and sleep routine for your newborn, you should plan that the last 1 to $1^1/2$ hours of your $2^1/2$-hour cycle will be for a nap. When moving to a 3-, $3^1/2$-, and in time, a 4-hour routine, your baby's naps will range anywhere from $1^1/2$ to $2^1/2$ hours.

NOTE: During the first two months, if your baby is not napping well, try cutting back on his waketime by 15-minute increments. Some babies become overstimulated during waketime and have difficulty settling in for a nap. The fatigued or overstimulated child becomes hyperalert—fighting off sleep through crying. If this is a regular problem for your baby, shorten his waketime.

There may be a brief period of fussing or crying when you put the baby down for a nap. Don't be deterred from doing what is best for the child. Some crying is a normal part of a baby's day and some babies will cry a few minutes in the process of settling themselves to sleep. The future trade-off will be a baby who goes down for a nap without fussing and wakes up cooing.

When settling for a nap, crying for 15 to 20 minutes is not going to hurt your baby physically or emotionally. Your baby will not lose brain cells, experience a drop in IQ, or have feelings of rejection that will leave him manic-depressive at age thirty. You do not undo all the love and care of the waking hours with a few minutes of crying. On the other hand, if you want a fussy baby, never let him cry, and hold, rock, and feed him as soon as he starts to fuss. We guarantee that you will achieve your goal.

Sleeping Patterns

Unlike feeding patterns, infant sleep behavior has more variation due to individual differences. Remember, stable sleep patterns are based on stable feed/wake patterns. When there are a number of changes in these two activities, there will be corresponding changes in his sleep patterns.

Newborn

Newborns can sleep sixteen to twenty hours per day, including the periods of sleep between each feeding. Under parent-directed feeding, this sleep will come in the form of six to eight naps (depending on the number of daily feedings). When your baby has been up for the appropriate duration, which may only be a total of forty-five minutes including feeding time, and she shows signs of fussiness, it is time for a nap.

Two Months

If you follow the principles of PDF, this will be the period when your baby drops his or her nighttime feeding and begins sleeping seven to eight hours continuously. Naps during the day should be at least 1 1/2 hours long. Seventy-five to 80 percent of PDF babies begin sleeping through the night on their own without any further parental guidance apart from routine feedings. It just happens. Some periods of night crying are experienced by the remaining 20 percent of children. Most of this takes place over a three-day period and the crying bouts average between five and thirty-five minutes in the middle of the night. On average, it takes three to five days for a nine-week-old to establish unbroken sleep cycles.

NOTE: It's not unusual for two- or three-month-old PDF babies to awaken at around 5:00 or 5:30 A.M. and talk to themselves for up to an hour. Afterward, they usually go back to sleep for another hour or so. This quirky phase can go on for a week or a month and sometimes longer. If you start to respond each time you hear a noise from the cradle, then 5:00 A.M. will become your baby's waketime—and yours, too.

Three to Five Months

During this period, your baby will drop his or her late-evening feeding, leaving four to six feeding periods during the day. Nighttime sleep will average ten to twelve hours. The baby will have three daytime naps between 1 1/2 to 2 hours in length, resulting in a longer waketime. Once the third nap is dropped, both waketime and often the other remaining naptimes will increase in duration.

Six to Sixteen Months

Your baby will drop his late-afternoon/early-evening nap at around six months of age, leaving two naptimes—one in the morning and one in the afternoon. The naps are usually about 1 1/2 to 2 hours long. (For more information on this period of development, please read *On Becoming Babywise II.*)

Sixteen Months and Older

Between sixteen and twenty months, the morning nap is dropped. Your baby should be sleeping ten to twelve hours at night and two to three hours during one afternoon nap.

Waking Up Happy

Between four and six months of age, infants generally develop a wake-up disposition—one that you highly influence. Your baby's disposition can be happy and content when you follow three basic rules for naps.

Rule 1: Mom, not baby, decides when the nap starts.

Rule 2: Mom, not baby, decides when the nap ends.

Rule 3: If your baby wakes up crying or cranky, it's most often because he or she has not had sufficient sleep. Other factors to consider are a dirty diaper, a noisy neighbor, sickness coming on, or an arm or leg stuck between the crib slats.

After having been put down for a nap, your baby will move from an active sleep state to relaxed sleep in thirty to forty-five minutes. In the next thirty to forty-five minutes, he or she will move from relaxed sleep back to active sleep. At the end of that cycle, your baby may begin to stir and cry. Parents often interpret this to mean naptime is over. Going in to pick up the baby, they assume the child's crankiness is his or her natural way of waking up. But that's not the case.

Remember, if your baby is waking up cranky or crying, he or she most likely is not getting enough sleep. Even though he or she may cry, your baby will probably go right back to sleep in ten minutes for another thirty to forty minutes of rest. When your baby gets enough sleep, you will notice a happy disposition; the baby will make happy cooing sounds, letting you know it's time to get him or her up.

Summary

When your baby starts to sleep through the night, people will invariably say, "You're just lucky," or "You've got an easy baby." Neither statement is true. Your baby is sleeping through the night because you trained him or her to do so. You can take the credit for your success. But do keep this fact in perspective: Getting your baby to sleep through the night is not the final goal of parenting—but we believe it does represent a right beginning.

Questions for Review

1. What common mistake is made in relation to waketime and naptime?

2. In the first month, your baby may be very sleepy. What are some things you can do to keep him or her awake?

3. In relation to the previous question, if your baby doesn't stay awake, what should you do?

4. Are naps optional for infants? Please explain.

5. When you follow a feeding, waketime, and sleeping routine, how much time should be devoted for a nap in a 3-hour cycle? In a 4-hour cycle?

6. Summarize the three "Wake Up Happy" rules.
    a.
    b.
    c.

7. What is the most common reason for your baby to wake up cranky or crying?

Chapter Eight

When Your Baby Cries

*Y*our baby cries and the world around you dims. You know that baby wants to tell you something. But what? Babies cry for many reasons. Why is hunger often the only one most people consider? Baby's cry should not be the day's unsolved mystery. Clearly, the cry is a multifunctional tool for baby to get what she needs. Besides crying when hungry, baby plays the blues when she is tired, wet, sick, bored, frustrated, out of the routine, fed too often, or sometimes simply because that is what normal, healthy babies do. Think of it as a signal, not a statement against your parenting. As mom or dad, learn to assess your baby's cry so you can respond properly. The ability to read your baby's cry will give you confidence in parenting. This puts you a full pace ahead of your own dear ol' aunt.

The Power of a Cry

Your baby's cry will have an enormous impact on his or her development. The cry alone will not shape him. The shaping factor is how you and the rest of your household respond to those cries. Throughout the day, your baby has a variety of specific needs for you to meet. Never before have baby's needs been so great. Suddenly, he must communicate them to you with the use of only one tool: the cry. Don't define his needs by the mere fact your baby is crying. Rather, learn to assess what each cry means. Assessment is critical to satisfying needs.

In early infancy, crying is an intuitive way of communicating both need and displeasure. Just as cries vary in purpose, intensity of baby's need also is reflected in the cry. The hunger cry is different from the sick cry. The sleepy cry is different from the "cuddle me" cry. And the distress cry differs from the demanding cry. Crying varies in volume, too. Sometimes a cry will be nothing more than a gentle whimper. Other times it is a violent protest. Attempts to minimize or block all crying can easily increase stress rather than decrease it. Emotional tears actually eliminate from the body chemically-activated stress hormones.

Most affected by a baby's cry are the parents. Though it is not unusual for grandparents to hedge them out in this regard, certainly no parent will take pleasure in his or her baby's cry. Neither will you, especially if you are a first-time parent. Baby's cry evokes emotions of uncertainty that you never knew before. You have never experienced such a powerful emotion—causing you to wonder if you have done something wrong. It's those ornery, unfamiliar feelings you are forced to experience inside yourself. This is your baby and this crying seems simply intolerable. If only you knew what to do. With a bit of effort, you can know.

The Inevitable Conflict

Should mom immediately offer her breast every time baby cries? Does this immediate response somehow instill love in baby's heart?

Then what about not responding to every cry with breast-feeding? Does this teach disappointment? Does the lack of immediate, ten-second response time create irreversible latent effects on personality development which surface years later, according to attachment theorists? We believe the answer to these questions is no. The question isn't whether crying is bad for your baby. The question is this: Will blocking baby's cry be good for him? The answer to this question also is no.

By blocking the cry, mother loses confidence in her own decision making. She also misses out on assessing the child's real needs. While she may be meeting a secondary cue, she probably is missing her baby's primary cues. The cue she is responding to is the *sound* of the cry. What mom needs to respond to is the *why* of the cry. Learn to assess the why behind baby's cry. Only then can your responses be rational and purposeful instead of emotive.

Whether it is blocking a baby's cry by offering food at each whimper or wearing baby in a sling all day to eliminate crying, beware. Indeed, babies who are allowed unlimited feedings, who are carried in a sling during the day, and who sleep with their mothers at night, do cry very little. This is true. However, this is not a result of love, training, and an abiding sense of security. Such babies cry less because this parenting philosophy calls for the suppression of all crying. Thus, greater value is placed on suppressing a child's cry than teaching good sleep habits. Try placing an "attached" baby in his own crib and in all probability there will be a great deal of crying.

How do feelings of security fit in? PDF babies move naturally from dependence to independence because the nature of the program fosters *relational security*. A baby's security is tied to his or her developing relationships with mom and dad, not simply the proximity of mom. The child who is physically attached to mom through baby slings and shared sleep is not necessarily experiencing relational attachment. That statement is easily proven. Just remove the child from mom at any point and observe how secure he or she appears. It's disheartening for a parent to see and hear her own child in a state of hysteria under the stress of independence.

Basic conditioning also plays into the mix. A mom who picks up her baby and offers the breast each time her baby cries is teaching her baby that food is the source of comfort, not mom. This explains why Marisa is not easily comforted by secondary caregivers. It may also help explain the obesity problem of our nation's youth and why so many adults turn to food for stress relief. They have been trained that way from the beginning. We are not trying to express an inevitable cause-and-effect relationship between a fat baby and a fat adolescent later on. However, poor eating habits in infancy may result in eventual obesity. Overfeeding or disregarding healthy eating patterns early on could be to blame.

There is another consideration. Babies not only become conditioned to being picked up at a whimper, but they also become abnormally dependent on it. A child like Marisa has been conditioned to expect immediate gratification. What will happen to Marisa when her parents no longer can satisfy her immediately? What happens when a second or third child comes into the family? Think of the emotional trauma both Marisa and mother will endure. This painful scenario is described by mothers as the child becoming "completely unglued." The child has been so conditioned to immediate response that he or she simply cannot cope with a delayed response. Now the child is emotionally fragile, rather than emotionally stable.

Marisa's mom has been bombarded by clichés: "You can't hurt a baby by picking her up whenever she cries." "You can't spoil her by loving her too much." Such clichés are clouds without water. The real issue is not a spoiled child but creating within the child a predisposition for immediate gratification. This becomes a destructive influence on her pretoddler and toddler development. Yes, you can hurt a baby by picking him or her up too much. Not in that single act, but in the collective nature of such a response. Over time this parenting attitude creates negative propensities. These inevitably spill over into pretoddler and toddler development.

Research has clearly demonstrated that immediate-gratification training negatively impacts a child's ability to learn, affecting the skills of sitting, focusing, and concentrating. All are prerequisites for academic advancement.[1]

These are facts. No evidence exists to prove that an immediate response to every cry teaches a baby about love. Likewise, there is no evidence proving that some crying fosters insecurity. A child learns love and gains security from the total context of the parent-child relationship. No single act or lack of one act provides this relationship.

The PDF Baby

Babies under the parent-directed feeding plan tend to cry less in the long run than babies who are demand fed. Why? Infants on a routine grow confident and secure in that routine. Their lives have order, and they learn the lesson of flexibility early in life.

Babies who settle into regular and predictable rhythms of activity develop greater tolerance to frustration and learn to use modes of communication other than crying. Chelsea expresses herself with happy sounds such as cooing and by excited body motions such as bouncing. These are additional modes of "baby talk."

Cries to Listen For

Some crying is normal. You need to expect it. However, you also need to stay alert to certain identifiable cries. For example, a high-pitched, piercing cry may be a signal of either internal or external bodily injury. Such a cry, if persistent, should be brought to the attention of your pediatrician.

A marked change in your baby's crying pattern may be a warning of illness. Look for a sudden increase in the frequency and duration of crying or a weak, mousy cry. Discuss this with your pediatrician. Cries indicating hunger or thirst are predictable with PDF babies. You can be certain the cry is not a hunger-and-thirst cry if your baby is satisfied after a feeding. With demand-fed babies, cries are unpredictable, leaving mom and dad guessing and anxious.

Babies who routinely cry and act hungry after an hour and a half are probably not getting enough food. If you are breast-feeding, check your milk supply and the factors which influence it. (See the section on testing your milk supply in chapter 6.) Another cry that needs investigation is when your baby wakes up in the middle of his nap with a loud, piercing cry. This could be caused by gas. Relief will come by burping your baby. Your baby may also be reacting to something in your breast milk as a result of what you ate earlier in the day. If this cry persists, physically check your baby. One mom reported that a strand of her long hair was wrapped tightly around her son's toe. Once the hair was gently removed, the crying stopped immediately.

Answering Your Baby's Cry

"How long should I let my baby cry?" This is the most common question asked by new moms. Answering isn't difficult, once you know how to identify both legitimate and illegitimate cry periods. The timing of your baby's cry is the first clue to understanding how you should respond. During the first four months of life, there are six possible cry periods. Three are classified as abnormal and three as normal.

Abnormal cry times include the following:
    a)   during feedings;
    b)   immediately after feedings;
    c)   at times when baby wakes early out of a sound nap.

Crying during any one of these periods requires attention. Don't wait for the crying to subside. Investigate it, looking for the root cause. These are not trainable cry periods, such as those times when you put your baby down for a nap. They come about due to legitimate need.

Crying during Feeding. Crying during feeding might occur if your baby isn't getting enough food or isn't taking in food fast enough. There could be a number of reasons for these conditions, including improper latching on or poor milk release. (Please see chapter 5, "Monitoring Your Baby's Growth.")

Crying Immediately after Feeding. If your baby cries routinely within thirty minutes after his or her feeding, and the cry sounds like a pain cry rather than a sleepiness cry, it may be caused by one of several factors:

1. *Trapped gas.* Young babies often swallow air during feedings. This air must be brought up again. Burp your baby by holding him or her against your shoulder, on your lap, or over your knee. Trapped gas is the first reason to consider when a baby wakes up thirty minutes into a nap. This cry is sometimes a high-pitched scream. If that is the case, pick the baby up, try burping and cuddling for a moment, then put the baby back down.

2. *Your diet.* If you are breast-feeding, consider what you are eating. Be careful to avoid eating too many dairy products or spicy foods. You don't have to completely eliminate these foods from your diet, but you may have to cut back considerably.

3. *A milk quality problem.* A breast-feeding mother can have a sufficient quantity of milk but at the same time not have a sufficient quality of milk. As a result, the baby responds with a hunger cry cue within an hour. Although this condition is relatively rare, it may affect as many as 5 percent of nursing mothers. What can you do to improve this condition? Check your diet and seek your pediatrician's counsel. He may recommend a nutritionist.

Waking Early Out of a Sound Nap. If your baby wakes out of a sound sleep with a strong cry, it may be the result of a combination of any of the three factors mentioned above. It might also mean you have too much flexibility in your routine.

Normal Crying Periods

Other than the abnormal cry periods just discussed (which always require your prompt attention), some crying is normal and should be expected. The normal cry periods are as follows:

a) just before feeding;

b) when baby is put down for a nap;

c) during the late afternoon/early evening period.

Crying Just before Feeding. Under normal circumstances, any crying that occurs just before a feeding should be limited, since the next event for the baby is mealtime. If your baby is hungry, feed him or her. If the child routinely shows signs of hunger before the next scheduled feeding, then find out why rather than letting the baby cry it out. Your baby's routine is to serve your baby and you. Neither of you should be enslaved to the routine.

Crying When Going Down for a Nap. When putting your baby down for a nap, the duration of crying is set by the child but monitored by the parent. Identifying and knowing your baby's cry patterns and disposition (personal style) will help you learn to discern real needs. Our first grandchild, Ashley, had a cry pattern at naptime that could easily be represented by a gradual bell curve. A gentle whimper built to a mild wail, which then would fall back again to a whimper. Sleep followed. The total time elapsed was ten minutes, with the exception of her late-afternoon cry, which lasted fifteen minutes.

By four weeks of age, it took Ashley just five minutes of crying to settle into her nap. Often she would be put down and fall right off to sleep. Knowing Ashley's cry patterns allowed her mother to be discerning one day when six-week-old Ashley cried longer than usual. Recognizing the difference in the length of the cry, Ashley's mother went in, picked her up, and held her for a moment. Then she put her back down. Ashley went off to a contented sleep.

Whitney is Ashley's sister. Her cry patterns were much different.

She would wail ten minutes, and then stop. About a minute later, she would wail ten minutes more. Then she would stop again. A moment after that she would whimper, then sleep. That naptime pattern lasted twelve weeks. Crying for Whitney became an art form, despite the fact that Whitney was nurtured, loved, and cared for with the same intensity as her sister. Whitney didn't have any more or less nutritional or love needs in her life, but she did have by nature a greater disposition for crying. Know your child's cry disposition and realize that some children have a greater propensity to cry. This is not necessarily a signal that their basic needs are not being met.

Our third grandchild, Katelynn, had yet a different history of crying. She would climb rapidly from a whimper to a wail, like an F-16 heading into the stratosphere. Then at the height of her cry, she would stop abruptly and drop off to a sound sleep. Her cry times averaged ten minutes in length at naptime for the first month. After four weeks, like her cousin Whitney, Katelynn became selective as to which naptimes she would cry. After three months, crying at naptime was rare for all three grandchildren. Instead, healthy, continuous naptime and nighttime sleep was the norm.

Without knowing your child's cry patterns, you will always be second-guessing his or her real need. You will never know how long your baby's cry period should last. You can't stand to hear baby cry? Join the club, but remember what's truly important. There's a purpose here. Without a goal in mind, i.e., teaching healthy sleep habits, letting your baby cry before falling asleep at naptimes makes little sense. The absence of an attainable and measurable goal breeds doubt and confusion. Why are you doing this uncomfortable thing? Who needs all the added stress? With the goal of teaching good sleep habits, some temporary crying is preferable over long-term poor sleep skills.

Some children cry fifteen minutes before falling asleep. Others vary the duration of their cry from five minutes at one naptime to an off-and-on, thirty-five-minute cry at another. If your baby cries longer than fifteen minutes, check on the baby. Pat him or her on the back, possibly holding the child for a moment. Then put the baby back down. Remember, you aren't training your child not to cry, but training him or her in the skill of sleep. This may be the only time in your baby's day that the practice of nonintervention is best.

The benefits of healthy sleep training come early. Expect a well-rested baby to be a good feeder. Also, you can put your baby down for his nap or bedtime and walk away. The child falls right to sleep and wakes with contentment. Another advantage to successful sleep training is that you may put your baby down at anyone's house and have the same success.

Crying During the Late Afternoon/Early Evening Period. Most babies have a personal fussy time. A fussy time in the late afternoon is not uncommon. That's true of both bottle- and breast-fed infants. There is no reason for you to be anxious about your fussy baby, because you are in good company. Literally millions of mothers and fathers are going through the same thing at nearly the same time each day.

If a child is not comforted by the baby swing, an infant seat, siblings, or grandma, consider the crib. At least there he has the chance of falling asleep. If you have a baby who becomes exceptionally and continuously fussy, consider the possibility that he is hungry. How is your milk supply? Are you eating right? Go back to chapter 4 and look at the factors influencing your milk production. Also, check what you are eating. Hot, spicy foods or a large intake of dairy products can be common contributors to a baby's fussy behavior at any time of day. Wrong foods in your diet easily amplify your baby's normal fussy time and create nightmares for young parents. It simply is not worth the aggravation. Learn to watch your intake.

Remember our cousins Chelsea and Marisa? Since Marisa lacks routine in her life, she is much more likely to be considered a fussy baby. Chelsea, on the other hand, may have a fussy time but will not be characterized as a twenty-four-hour fussy baby.

Don't misinterpret your baby's fussy time as colic. There is much disagreement as to the true origin of this overused condition. In Dr. Bucknam's medical practice and in testimonies from hundreds of former demand-feeding mothers, bouts of colic-like symptoms are substantially reduced with PDF. The last thing you should put into an irritated stomach is food. Yet that is usually the first thing many mothers do. The baby cries, and mom offers the breast. Baby's nursing is out of reflex, not the comfort found in more food.

Very few infants truly suffer from colic. Typically, spells of colic occur in the early evening, at night, and right after feeding. It can appear as early as baby's second week of life and usually disappears by the end of the twelfth week. You might see baby draw up his or her legs and clench fists tightly as if in pain. He or she may act hungry but begin crying partway through the feeding. If you observe these symptoms, contact your pediatrician. Having a child who cries for hours for no apparent reason can be extremely frustrating and emotionally draining on any parent. If your baby does suffer from colic, the best thing you can do is to keep that child on a routine. This allows his or her stomach to rest between feedings.

There is no precise time limitation for normal periods of crying.

Rather, think carefully about each cry situation. Determine when you should intervene and when you need to hold back. In time, and as a result of your training, your baby will go down for naps and night-time sleep without crying. These are children who actually look forward to sleep.

What Should I Do When My Baby Cries?

In relation to a baby's cry, the distinction between feeding philosophies is basic. Chelsea's mom understands the wisdom of first assessing her baby's cry and then acting. She listens, she thinks, and then she acts on her assessment.

Unfortunately, Marisa's mom will not take time to assess. In fact, she has been told it is best not to think. She simply reacts to her feelings when she hears her baby cry. Yet feelings never were and never will be the basis for any sound decision-making. Why would intuition suddenly assume center stage in this, her most critical role? Crying is a mechanism given by the Creator. For babies, it is one of the few ways they have to let us know of a need. What crying does for the parent hearing it is to arouse emotions that in turn stimulate the thought process leading to assessment. Mother's decisions without assessment can be dangerous. To deny the importance of careful assessment is to deny parents their role as leader. Leaders must be clear-headed and ready to make decisions. They should not be driven by their emotions.

In practice, emotional mothering can set the stage for child abuse. How? It creates a vicious cycle. A common characteristic found among abusive parents is a tendency to direct thoughtless, impassioned responses toward their innocent children. Too often those responses are fueled by sleepless nights and a child trained to be demanding.

How should you respond when your baby cries? Unless you sense your baby is in danger, take a moment to listen and assess his or her crying. After a brief assessment, take the appropriate action. Here are some practical and somewhat more detailed steps to follow.

Listen for the Type of Cry. Even in the early days and weeks, you will begin to distinguish different tones and patterns in your baby's crying. Simply stop and listen. You may find that the crying ends as quickly as it began. By listening you can determine a right response. If a child has a dirty diaper, are you going to feed him or her? Of course not. If your baby has trapped gas, is food the answer? Never. If your baby cries because of an ear infection, is nursing what the baby needs? Hardly. Your baby is working hard to spell out his or her needs. Get to know your baby by decoding baby's cries.

Think about where your baby is in his or her routine. Is naptime finished or is your baby in the middle of his or her nap, in need of resettling? Does your baby need to go down for a nap? Has she been in the swing too long? Did he lose his toy? Did she spit up? Is this your baby's fussy time of day? This is only a short list of why your baby might be crying. Many reasons other than hunger can just as quickly turn on the tears.

Take action based on what you have heard and reasonably concluded. Just remember, sometimes the best action is no action at all. For example, if your baby is clean, fed, and ready for naptime, let him or her learn how to fall asleep alone. This may be precisely what your baby needs. If you try to nurse your child to sleep, you have only succeeded in manipulating his or her sleep. In the long run, you are digging for yourself that big, black hole of endless sleepless nights into the toddler years.

Take note of how long your baby cries. After watching the clock just one time, many moms have been shocked to learn that the seemingly endless bout of shrieking lasted all of five to ten minutes. In the event that you have listened, waited, and determined that the crying is not subsiding, gather more information by checking on the baby. Peek into his or her crib and see if your baby has become jammed into a corner. In that case you simply move your baby and offer a gentle pat on the back before leaving the room.

There will be times when your assessment calls for picking up and holding your baby. You simply may need to reassure the child that everything is all right. Sometimes there is no rhyme or reason behind the need for special time in mommy's arms. Your assessment may produce many options. However, blocking your child's cry because you can't handle it should not be up for consideration.

When Should I Hold and Comfort My Baby?

You will, of course, hold your baby many hours each day. As you care for and feed your baby, holding and cuddling him comes naturally. Flirt with baby. Rock him in your arms. Sing a sweet song to your infant. Happy or not so happy, baby loves the attention. Wouldn't you? Understand, though, that constantly holding baby during every fussy time is easily overdone.

Parents should offer comfort when comfort is needed, but stay mindful of this basic question: What type of comfort should I give my baby right now? A diaper change will comfort a wet baby. A feeding will comfort a hungry baby. Holding will comfort a startled baby, and sleep will comfort a tired baby. A baby can receive comfort in many ways and from different people. Certainly dad, older siblings, grandma, and grandpa can be sources of comfort. Also, comfort for baby comes by being held, rocked, sung to, taken for a stroller ride, or placed near a source of music.

The good news for baby is that mom's breasts are not the only source of comfort. Mom, too, finds peace in this reality. Wisdom dictates that a mother should recognize that a baby responds to different forms of comfort at different times. If you use one source exclusively—nursing, for example—you are not necessarily comforting your baby, only stopping the baby's cry by arousing the sucking reflex. If nursing is the only form of comfort, too often real needs are missed.

Summary

As a parent, learn to recognize your baby's different cries. Trust in this knowledge. Then, confidently respond to your infant. A wise parent will listen, think, and then take action. Don't get caught up in the watchful gazes of those on the sidelines. With effort and understanding, parent from the wisdom you have gathered. Remember, as baby grows her patterns of crying may change. Your baby may be fed, clean, dry, and healthy, when one day she begins to cry before falling asleep. Consider this just one more phase of your child's normal development.

Questions for Review

1. Throughout the day your baby will have definite needs for you to meet. What are the right and wrong ways to define those needs?

2. What are parents teaching an infant when they pick him or her up and offer food each time the baby cries? What problems can result from this practice?

3. List the three abnormal and normal cry periods. What is the general difference between the two?

4. State what is wrong with this advice: "When your baby cries, don't think. Just react."

5. What three things should you do when your baby cries?
   a.

   b.

   c.

6. As it relates to comforting a baby, what is the standard question every parent should ask? Give examples.

Chapter Nine

Multiple Birth:

The Endless Party

a baby is a great blessing, and multiple births represent multiplied blessings to parents. But with twins, triplets, or quadruplets, your joy will be accompanied by a great deal of work. This is a matter of simple addition. (No, make that multiplication!)

All parenting requires organization and thinking ahead. However, when you bring home a multiple birth, you really have to think and plan, because when the unexpected happens, it happens in multiples. People with a single baby make their mistakes one at a time; parents of triplets often make their mistakes in triplicate. On the bright side, when you do things right, you have success in multiples, too.

At our house we like to think of parenting our triplets as the party that never ends. When our three boys were tiny preemies and needed feeding every three hours, we saw feeding times as an opportunity for family fun and fellowship. The feeders would sit together in the same room and discuss their day, tell jokes or stories, or sing songs. Even at 3 A.M., we feeders were encouraged in our toil by our mutual commitment to see this as an opportunity to socialize.

From the earliest age, children will sense your attitude. If you approach their care as if it is a burden or drudgery, then your children will respond in a burdensome way and you will experience drudgery. Instead, see each day as an adventure and know that each stage of your children's development is precious.

Bringing Them Home

Multiple-birth pregnancies are at high risk for prematurity. Therefore a major challenge early on is that of caring for tiny babies in multiple. Your babies may stay in the hospital neonatal intensive care unit (NICU) for a while. They will probably come home one at a time as they reach safe weights and develop sucking skills. They may come home with apnea and heart monitors in tow. (The apnea monitor provides assurance a child is breathing.)

Cribs. When your babies are very young, they won't be moving around much on their own. It's perfectly acceptable to put two or even three small babies in the same crib. We suggest you separate them when they are mature enough to wiggle around in the crib, preventing any baby from becoming a suffocation risk to another.

Diapers. As a prospective parent, you may have read exhaustive articles in newspapers and periodicals on the merits of disposable diapers versus cloth diapers. All combined, triplets will use between twenty-four and thirty diapers a day. So with multiples, the cost of diapers can become a significant item on the household budget. Weigh your options. For lowest cost up front, you would buy cloth diapers and wash them yourself. But when you factor in the need for daily loads of laundry, the cost in terms of time and inconvenience is considerable. Also, cloth can have a hidden cost built in due to increased incidence of diaper rash. And babies can't go as long between diaper changes in cloth as they can in disposable diapers, because of the lower absorbency of cloth diapers and their higher discomfort level when wet. Parents of multiples can find it hard enough to keep track of who has been changed and who is due for a fresh diaper—let alone be aware of who is wet or dirty at an unexpected time.

Disposable diapers are nice because babies don't experience discomfort even when a wet diaper is overlooked. On the other hand, commercial diaper services are cheaper than disposable diapers. But remember, you will have multiple quantities of wet, smelly diapers waiting for pickup each week. My personal preference is for disposable diapers but because of cost concerns, I encourage parents to try a diaper service and see if they can keep the babies changed and comfortable; if this service works for you, you may realize significant savings.

You Need Help

As I counsel parents of multiples, the single worst mistake I see them make is to assume they can handle this challenge on their own. Frequently, the budget is small and hired help is out of the question, so mom and dad set out to accomplish all child care duties on their own. Don't make this mistake! You can't do it alone.

You don't necessarily have to spend money to get help. There are several alternatives. Extended family members often love to help out—especially if your babies are eating and sleeping on a schedule. Some high schools, colleges, seminaries, and yeshivas near your home may offer classes in childhood development. Your home could become a learning lab for a kindhearted student. Churches and synagogues are filled with people available to lend a helping hand—you need only ask. If one or more of your children comes home using monitors, you may be a candidate for in-home nursing care at the state's expense. To find out about this possibility, check with the social worker associated with the neonatal intensive care unit of your hospital or your pediatrician.

When someone asks if they can help, always say "Yes, please!" Keep a daily planner handy so you can give all who offer help an exact date and time they can serve you, right there on the spot; and immediately assign them a job. You may want help with baby care or, if your volunteers have limited time, ask them to help with your weekly errands—the laundry, post office, grocery store, pharmacy, and so on. Delegating is one of the keys to preserving your sanity with multiples.

Let's Talk about Feeding

Are you going to breast-feed? A mother of multiples often can breast-feed. Whether this is the right choice for you and your babies is entirely up to you and your children to determine. Much will depend on your babies' maturity at birth and whether or not they require NICU care; whether or not you had a cesarean section; and how many babies you have. Mothers of twins are more successful at breast-feeding than mothers of triplets. If your babies come right home with you from the hospital, it will be much easier to establish a breast-feeding pattern.

As explained in chapter 4, a mother's milk is a complete and perfect food. It is easily digested, provides excellent nutrition, and contains the right balance of proteins and fats. It also provides additional antibodies that are necessary for establishing your baby's early immune system. If your babies are in the NICU, even if you don't plan to breast-feed them directly, you may want to provide milk for them using an electric breast pump. Many pediatricians recommend this and insurance companies will often reimburse a mother for the pump rental while the baby is in the NICU. Premature babies are especially in need of their mother's antibodies that are provided in breast milk.

Each of your babies is different. You may plan to breast-feed all of them but find that one prefers the bottle to the breast. Some moms successfully breast-feed all of their multiples in a rotating fashion, with one baby receiving a bottle each feeding while the others have a turn at the breast. Other mothers produce enough milk to feed all three of their triplets. A good electric pump is very helpful in establishing and maintaining a milk supply for multiples. You may be able to pump after you feed one or two babies so that a third or fourth baby can receive breast milk in a bottle. Breast-feeding can be magnificently easy once established and learned by mom and babies, but it doesn't start out easy, especially after the stress of a high-risk pregnancy. Please relax your expectations of yourself and get good counsel from a professional lactation consultant. Breast-feeding a multiple birth may not come naturally and you probably will need some counsel.

If your newborn babies are low birth weight and/or premature, they will probably sleep all the time. You may find they hardly ever wake up, sleeping even when you are changing their diapers, bathing them, and feeding them. Premature babies react unexpectedly to stimulus by withdrawing and sleeping. Don't fight their sleepiness. Do your best to get the food into them but don't try for more than thirty minutes every three hours. By this I mean that from the beginning of one feeding to the beginning of the next, no more than three hours should elapse. Attempt to feed and burp each infant for thirty minutes, putting the sleeping baby back to bed for the remaining 2 1/2 hours of the cycle. Do this even if the baby was sucking ineffectively and only received a fraction of the usual feeding amount or when a significant amount of the feeding is spit back up. I recommend that you don't refeed after a baby spits up if the thirty-minute limit is up. If the baby spits up ten minutes or so into the feeding, try refeeding until the time is up.

One important aspect of feeding newborn and premature infants is a good assessment of their hydration. Each baby should have between six and eight wet diapers each day. If you are breast-feeding, this will be one clue to help you determine that they are properly latched on and consuming adequate quantities of milk. But with a multiple birth, especially three or more babies, keeping track of who has had a wet diaper and who hasn't can become a challenge. Especially in the first sleep-deprived postpartum weeks, you can lose track of even obvious things. So write it all down. Keep your "Healthy Baby Growth" charts near the changing table and keep them updated. Consider color coding them, assigning a different color to each child. This will make it easier to keep track of each child's progress.

As your babies mature, feedings will become easier and you will probably be able to feed each baby in under thirty minutes. Adhere closely to the feeding time/waketime/naptime order for each baby.

When one wakes at night to eat, wake them all and feed them. However, when one wakes up early from a nap, resist the temptation to reward the baby with a feeding. Instead, check for a dirty diaper, calm the baby, and lead the child into comforting himself or herself and going back to sleep.

Let's Talk About Sleep

Sleeping for multiples is crucial to your peace of mind and to their happiness. With newborns—especially two or more small, premature babies—the temptation is to focus on how much they eat, how often they eat, and whether or not they are gaining weight consistently. My husband and I have applied the *Babywise* principles from birth on with our triplets, and we have counseled many parents of multiples to do the same. It has become clear that the true key to eating and weight gain is sleep. If you want your children to eat and to grow, then teach them to sleep. A rested baby will eat. An exhausted, agitated, sleep-deprived baby will howl, fuss, suck ineffectively, and spit up repeatedly.

You may be afraid your babies will wake up hungry an hour after you put them down if they have not taken a full feeding. The surprise is that they won't wake up hungry before the next feeding but will probably wake up just in time for the next scheduled feeding, better rested and ready to eat a full bottle. Overall, the newborn baby whose parents focus on sleep rather than on calories consumed will get more nutrition because he or she will be better rested, have better digestion, and be ready to suck strongly.

As your multiples mature, they will develop definite waketimes and sleep times. When they are newborn or premature, they will always fall asleep while you are feeding them, or maybe they won't even wake up for the feeding. As they get older, they will still get drowsy with feedings but with a little stimulation you can have them fully awake and ready to play after a meal. Waketime activities with multiples should always include some independent playtime. When the appointed time for the nap arrives, the babies may indicate readiness by being fussy and undistractable or they may be wide awake and cheery. Put them down awake! It will be clear that logistically you can't rock two, three, or more babies to sleep at each naptime. Your babies need to learn to comfort themselves. Multiple babies, even more than singletons, need to learn patience and how to calm themselves. The fact that mommy and daddy each have only one lap and one set of arms sets up some unavoidable limits. Self-comforting is particularly important when they are sick or under stress. If babies have learned the skill of sleep early on in life they will seek sleep when they feel tired instead of further stressing themselves with crying and fussing.

If your multiple babies have been sharing a room since birth, they won't wake each other up. They will learn to shut out each other's crying, so don't separate them when one is fussing. When little ones are having a particularly hard cry, you can go in every ten minutes and pat them, reassure them, and possibly check for a wet or soiled diaper. You will function as a guide, teaching them how to self-comfort. Go in to them only long enough to cause them to stop crying but not long enough for them to fall asleep. Your goal is to put them down awake, allowing them to fall asleep on their own—without a transition process, such as rocking or patting. This can be more challenging than it sounds, due to the sheer physical effort of caring for multiples.

You need to start and finish each eat/wake/sleep cycle in a fairly structured fashion. It takes about fifteen to twenty minutes to pick up three babies, diaper them, and put them in their cribs for a nap. One common pitfall for parents is to allow their babies to fall asleep in their waketime activity chairs or swings. Parents get busy doing a household chore, answering the phone, or trying to solve one baby's problem, only to find the others have fallen asleep sitting up. While it's true they've fallen asleep by themselves, they didn't do this in the right place—their own cribs. If this happens often, they may develop difficulty self-comforting as they lie in their cribs. There will always be unexpected events to contend with, but try to plan ahead by putting your babies down awake in their cribs when you are not distracted. That way, when they do fall asleep sitting up, it will be a rare event and not a habit.

Regarding sleep, the number one multiple question I field is this: "The babies are four months old adjusted age. They are feeding every four hours but not sleeping through the night. Why?" I have to console these moms back to a rigorous three-hour feeding schedule during the day and encourage them to push sleep at night. This usually results in a "miraculous" call three days later to report that one or all the babies are now sleeping eight hours at night.

Here is the first rule governing nighttime sleep. Do not be tempted to lengthen the time between daytime feeding until your babies are sleeping at least nine to ten hours at night. They need the every-three-hour feeding during the day to distinguish night from day but also to make sure all their nutritional needs are being met. A basic three-hour routine will accomplish both.

As they continue to mature, a brand-new problem arises:

Between six and nine months of age, your babies will discover each other. This is where the party really begins! Now your problem is that they are having too much fun entertaining each other. They won't wake up to each other's crying but will wake up to each other's laughter and carrying on. They have built-in buddies. What helps in this situation is to have a toy that can be played with quietly in bed while a baby's siblings continue to sleep. In our family we used Busy-Box-type activity toys. Other families place small, noiseless toys in each child's bed after the children have fallen asleep so the baby who wakes up can play quietly and independently with the toy.

Strongly discourage your multiples from getting out of their cribs on their own. All babies should stay in their cribs until given permission, but for multiples there is an additional safety issue—the threat one aggressive toddler poses to another when unsupervised. We convinced our triplets that climbing in and out of their cribs was impossible without the help of a stepladder. When the stepladder was not available, they didn't get in and out of their cribs. They slept in their cribs until after their third birthday without any episodes of unauthorized entry or exit.

Routine for Multiples

The routine of each baby shouldn't vary, but the eat/sleep schedule of your multiple-birth babies with respect to one another may be impacted by many factors. How many babies are there? How many feeders are there? Are you breast-feeding? Each baby should have feeding time, waketime, and naptime. Don't change that order, except for late-night feedings when there is no waketime, and for premature babies who aren't neurologically mature enough to tolerate waketime.

If you have triplets and there is only one caregiver for them most of the time, you may choose to stagger your babies' schedules. Here's how this might work: The feeder (probably you) starts the process on the hour with baby A, finishes half an hour later and goes on to baby B, while baby A has waketime in a bouncy seat nearby. At the top of the next hour, baby C wakes for feeding and baby A is ready for naptime. When all three babies are fed there is an hour and a half of non-feeding time before the cycle starts again. If there are two feeders in your home, you could always have two babies eating at the same time.

With more help, all babies in a home with triplets or twins can be on approximately the same schedule. With two helpers, three babies can eat at the same time. Because babies eat at different speeds, there will be a fast eater and a slow eater. Once you figure out who eats slowest and who fastest, you can establish a system whereby one helper feeds the slow eater while the second helper feeds the fastest eater and the in-between eater. A breast-feeding mom can feed two babies at the same time while someone gives a bottle to the third baby.

Older bottle-fed babies can be propped up and fed two at a time or even three at a time, but you can't prop up bottles for premature babies or small babies who are having difficulty learning to suck.

Waketime

You won't need to focus on waketime during the first weeks your babies are home, but soon they will stay awake for the whole feeding and begin to take an interest in the world around them. A reclining upright seat is the perfect place to put a baby for these early wake-time periods. The seat allows the baby to look around and wave arms and legs while still upright, while at the same time discouraging them from spitting up—a common occurrence in babies who are lying horizontally. Reclining seats are useful later for feeding with a propped-up bottle or for beginning solids when the babies are still too small for high chairs. A word of caution: never leave a baby unattended in a seat.

Waketime activity for multiples doesn't require that you have three of everything. Babies tire of most activities after ten to twenty minutes, so you can set up rotating "stations." One baby is in the wind-up swing while another plays with a rattle in the playpen; the third is in the bouncy seat playing with a different rattle or sitting with mommy singing a song and playing one on one. At fifteen-minute intervals, you rotate the babies to the next activity.

Individual time is essential to happy multiples. They need independent play time each day, and they also need individual, one on one time with mommy and daddy. By necessity we tend to think of multiples as a unit. We feed, change, dress, and bathe them all at the same time. It's much easier to make sure you are being fair and that everyone's needs are being met if you keep the babies on a schedule and do all major daily activities collectively. How you structure wake-time and the way you plan the babies' play activities can offer a break from the monotony of cookie-cutter baby care. Leave all but one of the babies with your spouse or a helper and take just one for a walk or on an errand to the store. Or read just one a story while the others play independently.

As multiples enter toddlerhood, they find themselves in a world where there is always someone else their size grabbing at them or at the toy they are about to pick up. Time in a playpen for a multiple becomes a time of refuge. They can do whatever they want there without someone interrupting them and taking their things. You can have one of nearly every other piece of equipment, but multiple playpens—one for each child—is a good early investment. Playpen time also provides a welcome relief for mommy: she can answer the phone or make lunch while the children play safely. Begin to practice playpen time at three to four months of age. Start with just ten minutes a day and slowly increase the time, so that by one year of age, they can stay in the playpen for at least forty minutes.

A Word to Husbands

The key to harmonious family life is the primacy of the husband-wife relationship. All other relationships in the home are impacted—positively or negatively—by the health and success of the husband-wife relationship. You will only be as good a parent as you are a spouse. For this reason, it's even more essential with multiples that dad help out. Your wife will only be able to listen to, share, and enjoy you if she feels your support and encouragement. Your wife is the chief feeder, diaper-changer, bather, and entertainer of a multiple birth. She has no "down time." Twenty-four hours a day she has to be calm and controlled, so she can make the important assessments and decisions that are part of the babies' daily life. The more you cherish and serve her, the more you will get back in the form of a composed, wise mom and peaceful, secure children.

Chapter Ten

Problem Solving

*Y*ou feed, cuddle, and bathe your baby. A diaper change here and a rattle shake there. Is this the extent of life with baby? Only if baby is the store-bought variety, complete with two outfits and a bottle of disappearing milk. No, your baby is unlike any other. She is alive, a complete person with complex needs. There is no disc or cassette to insert for proper behavior. She cannot be programmed according to any book or theory. Certainly, raising baby brings an abundance of joy. Yet intermingled with outstanding moments of accomplishments in parenting are the challenges, the unknown realm of creative parenting opportunities.

Here we explore some questions commonly asked by PDF parents. Some of our answers simply review what has been covered. Other situations will be unique, requiring additional information in the answer. Do not wait for a challenging situation to arise before reading through this section. These questions can prevent as many problems as they solve and serve as an excellent review of *On Becoming Babywise*. Let's begin with the first week of life.

Week One

1. How soon after birth can I implement PDF?

Mentally, you begin immediately. In practice, however, you should ease yourself into the program. For the first few days, just relax. Actual implementation for breast-feeding moms begins anytime between day one and day seven. We recommend this gradual transition whether you demand feed, follow a strict schedule, or observe the flexibility found in PDF. Take those first few days to get acquainted with baby and become accustomed to your new role as mom, the caregiver of life. Enjoy getting acquainted with your child, and work your way into the PDF plan at your own speed. By the end of the first week your baby will be ready to cooperate with your guidance, and you will be ready to cooperate with meeting his or her love and nutritional needs.

However, you are not completely off the hook. As mom, you have a couple of basic goals to accomplish. The best place to start is with feeding and time guidelines. In feeding, concentrate on getting baby to take a full meal. No nibbling to tide him over. You also want to work on getting a minimum of eight such feedings in a 24-hour period. If you can accomplish this, you will most likely find that your baby falls into a predictable three-hour routine by day seven. From there you start working on establishing your baby's feed/wake/sleep cycles if they're not already in place.

2. When my baby is brought to me for his very first feeding, how long should I let him nurse?

If possible, nurse your baby soon after birth. Within the first hour and a half is best, since newborns are usually most alert at this time. Strive for fifteen minutes per side, with a minimum ten minutes on each breast. This time frame will allow for sufficient stimulation. Remember to position the baby properly. This is critical to both baby's and your success. If your baby wants to nurse longer during this first feeding, allow him to do so. In fact, with the first several feedings, you can go as long as the two of you are comfortable. However, be sure both breasts are stimulated at each feeding.

3. What will my feeding routine look like over the next several days?

Throughout the next three to five days, maintain your basic 2½- to 3-hour feeding routine. Nurse between fifteen and twenty minutes per side at each of these feedings. This means your average nursing period lasts from thirty to forty minutes this first week. Here's where the work begins. You want to try keeping baby awake at the breast. You want your baby taking full feedings as opposed to snacking. Full feedings are the key to success both in terms of early lactation and establishing a healthy routine. It is our experience that mothers who work to get a full feeding during the first week have babies who naturally transition into predictable three-hour routines within seven to ten days.

4. My baby wants to sleep more than eat. What do I do?

This is fairly common. During those early days your baby can be quite sleepy. Sleep alone is no problem. Missed feedings are. If you find your baby's sleep is interfering with your efforts to feed on routine, consider the following actions.

- Unwrap your baby before feeding if he is wrapped or swaddled in a blanket. Swaddled babies tend to sleep longer periods.
- Avoid water or formula supplements unless directed by your pediatrician. Also, avoid pacifiers during the first week.
- Do not let your baby sleep longer than three hours during week one. Sleeping skills are not the priority this first week. Adequate lactation must take top billing.
- Gently stroke a cool washcloth on your baby's face, forehead, neck. No guilt. Remember, full feedings represent your baby's best interests. The cool cloth is a means toward this end.
- Vary your nursing position. Instead of the cuddle hold, try the side-lying position. Check to see that baby is latched on properly.
- Get your baby to take full feedings.
- If feeding doesn't go well, wait thirty to forty-five minutes and try again.
- Call your pediatrician if your baby acts lethargic, is not eating every three hours, or is not stooling.

5. My baby has jaundice. Should I offer water between feedings?
Your pediatrician will direct the appropriate treatment for jaundice and use of liquid supplements. However, breast milk is the best liquid cure for jaundice. In some cases more frequent breast-feeding is necessary. Possibly for a couple of days you might feed every two hours. That's okay. The situation here calls for this adjustment and should be only temporary.

6. How do I know if my baby is getting enough food in that first week before my milk comes in?

Check his diaper. That's right. A healthy stooling pattern is a positive indicator of adequate nutrition during that first week. Newborn stools in the first week transition from the first greenish black and sticky stool, called meconium, to a brownie batter transition stool. This stool then transitions to a mustard yellow stool. After the first week, look for two to five or more yellow stools each day along with seven to eight wet diapers. These all add up to indicate baby is getting what she needs.

Weeks Two through Eight

1. My baby seems to have her days and nights mixed up. She sleeps long stretches during the day and has her alert time at night. How do I fix it?

Unless you are willing to pull an all-nighter, you need a proactive plan. Parent-directed feeding has what you need to get baby in sync with reality. Wake your baby and feed her at three-hour intervals during the day. This is where PDF differs from demand-feeding advice. With the PDF plan, helping your child organize his feeding and sleep times is a prerequisite to organizing his days and nights. That is why we advise that you start with a preset time for the first morning feeding. From there, wake your sleeping baby and feed her. Then at night, let her wake naturally. However, during the first six weeks (preferably eight), breast-fed babies should not be allowed to sleep longer than five hours at night before offering a feeding.

2. My baby is fussy between 9:00 P.M. and 11.00 P.M. What's wrong?

Probably nothing. Every baby has a personal fussy time. For most, fussing occurs in either late afternoon or early evening. This is true for both bottle- and breast-fed infants. If you experience this, you have an abundance of company. Literally millions of mothers and fathers are going through the same thing at just about the same time each day.

If a child is not comforted by the baby swing, an infant seat, sibling, grandma, or you, consider the crib. At least there he may fall asleep. If you have a baby who becomes exceptionally and continuously fussy, consider the possibility he is hungry. How is your milk supply? Are you eating right? Go back to chapter 4 and look at the factors influencing your milk production.

Also, review what you're eating. Hot, spicy foods or a large intake of dairy products or caffeine may contribute to baby's fussiness. This can happen at any time of the day. The presence of wrong foods in your diet can amplify your baby's normal fussy time and create nightmares for young parents. So, turn a cold shoulder to the ice cream. Forgo the nachos and make a list of all the foods you'll soon enjoy when baby no longer needs your milk.

Remember Chelsea and Marisa? Marisa never had the advantage of routine. She is far more likely to be fussy than her cousin Chelsea. Immediately integrated into the PDF plan, Chelsea still may have that fussy time but overall will not be characterized as a fussy baby.

Don't misinterpret your baby's fussy time as colic. Defining colic has met with much disagreement. In Dr. Bucknam's medical practice and hundreds of testimonies from former demand-feeding mothers, bouts of colic-like symptoms are substantially reduced with PDF. In a typical scenario, baby cries and mother offers the breast. Yet, the last thing you should put into an upset stomach is food. When this is mom's first response, baby nurses purely out of reflex.

True colic appears as early as the second week and usually disappears by the end of the twelfth week. Spells of colic are typical in the early evening, at night, and right after feeding. Baby may draw up his or her legs and clench the fists tightly as if in pain. While baby may act hungry, he or she begins crying partway through the feeding. If these symptoms occur, contact your pediatrician. A child who cries for hours without apparent cause can be emotionally draining on you as a parent. You need loving support. If your baby does suffer from colic, the best thing you can do is keep the child on a routine. This will allow his or her stomach to rest between feedings.

Avoid overstimulating your baby. Excessive rocking and bouncing might contribute to this. Also, avoid holding your baby while watching television. While baby may appear fascinated by your local anchors' account of daily events, most likely his brain will go into overload. The rapid changing of light patterns from scene to scene along with the change in volume can heighten baby's tension. He neurologically cannot handle such rapid light and sound changes.

3. My two-week-old daughter nurses on one side, then falls asleep. One hour later, she wants to eat again. What should I do?

If she is hungry, feed her, but work on keeping your baby awake to take a full feeding from both breasts. Here are some ideas: Change her diaper between sides; undress her; rub her head or feet with a cool, damp washcloth. Do what you must to keep her awake. Then, finish the task at hand. Baby must eat. If you allow baby to snack, she won't argue with that. Babies learn very quickly to become snackers if you let them. If your baby increasingly becomes characterized by snacking, you must work on stretching the times between feedings to make the $2^{1}/_{2}$-hour minimum.

4. My three-week-old baby starts to cry one hour after his last feeding and appears hungry. I've tried to stretch his time but can't get him to go longer. What's the problem?

If baby is hungry, feed him. Then, spend some time investigating the probable cause of his uncooperative stance. Most often, a baby fails to make the $2^{1}/_{2}$-hour minimum (especially babies over two weeks of age) because the order of daytime activities is reversed. The order of events must be feeding time, waketime, then naptime. When a baby goes only two hours between feedings, it's usually due to the reversal of the last two activities. Are you letting baby drift off to sleep immediately after feeding? Also, check your milk supply. As we stated earlier, if your baby is hungry, feed him. But investigate why he is not reaching the minimum mark and start working toward it. Check your healthy baby growth chart for signs of adequate nutrition.

5. My three-week-old baby is waking up after only 30 minutes of naptime. We're keeping her up for 1 to $1^{1}/_{2}$ hours of waketime. Should we try to keep her up longer?

There are two common reasons for this. She either needs to burp or was overstimulated before going to sleep. If burping is the cause, get her up and gently work on releasing that uncomfortable bubble. Once you recognize the need for this and learn to achieve success in burping, this problem is solved.

However, if overstimulation is the culprit, you must determine how this is happening. Perhaps your baby is being excessively carried, bounced, played with, or just kept awake too long in hopes of tiring her out. These efforts usually backfire because of your baby's immature neurological system. Some babies, especially preemies, handle over-stimulation by neurologically shutting down. What appears to be sleep is not sleep at all but a self-protective neurologic strategy. Certainly, you must hold, rock, and play with your baby. Just be certain that your efforts are not excessive in the early weeks. Babies, as well as children, do not nap well if overly stimulating activities precede naptime.

6. Sometimes right after I feed my baby, she spits up what looks to be a good amount of the feeding. Should I feed her again right away?

Your baby may seem to have lost her whole meal and then some. At 3 A.M., it might look even worse. Actually, the amount of partially digested milk spit up often appears to be greater than its true volume. Normally you won't feed her again until her next routine feeding. Overfeeding and doing a poor job of burping a baby are common causes for projectile vomiting. Try paying closer attention to these details. However, if this problem persists, it may signal a digestive problem. For your own peace of mind and possibly your baby's health, contact your pediatrician.

7. Occasionally, just after I have fed, changed, and played with my baby, I will put him down for a nap and within five minutes he starts crying—hard. This is unusual for him. What should I do?

Check on your baby. Since this is not routine behavior, it calls for your attention. He may simply have a messy diaper or need to be burped. Also bear in mind that at naptime some crying is not unusual. Napping is a skill. It needs to be learned. Avoid the myth that your baby is signaling a need to be held and rocked every time he cries.

8. My three-week-old breast-fed baby has started to sleep through the night already. Is that okay?

NO! This is not acceptable for a breast-fed baby. We prefer you feed your baby at least once at night until he is at least five weeks old. Some babies have a greater propensity to sleep through the night early. If you have a baby like this and if he or she is gaining well and has good urine output (seven to eight wet diapers per day), then early nighttime sleep may be acceptable. If this is your baby, continue to monitor the daily healthy growth signs. Even at six weeks, make sure your breast-fed baby does not go longer than eight hours at night. In this case, you would maintain at least seven to eight good feedings during the day. A bottle-fed baby may sleep through the night sooner, but you must monitor all healthy growth indicators during the day.

9. My baby is ten weeks old and has not yet slept through the night. What should I do to eliminate the middle-of-the-night feeding?

You have several options before you. First, go back and review the specific guidelines listed in chapter 6. Are you following them? Second, do nothing for a couple of weeks. Ninety-seven percent of all PDF babies achieve the ability to sleep through the night by then on their own. Third, keep track of the exact times your baby is waking. If he is waking every night at basically the same time, then he is waking out of habit rather than need. In this case, you may choose to help him eliminate the feeding period. Normally it takes three nights before the wake habit is broken and is usually accompanied by some crying. Be assured, your baby will not remember those nights. What you will recall in days, months, and years to come is the healthy, happy baby that is well-rested and not the few nights of testing that got you there. Helping baby learn this behavior has positive long-term effects on you both.

10. I recently was at a family gathering and had just put the most popular guest (my baby daughter) down for a nap. She began to cry, and everyone looked to see what I would do. Aunt Martha, visiting from out of town, volunteered to get the baby back up and I reluctantly agreed to let her. What should I have done?

This answer depends on the age of your baby. If you are characterized by following a routine, then allow Aunt Martha to get the baby. A three-week-old may fall asleep very comfortably in Aunt Martha's arms, and that will be fine for this one visit. If the baby is six months old, then let Aunt Martha know that her favorite niece will be up and ready to give love in two hours. Remember, unplanned disruptions will come into your day. Count on it. But also take comfort in knowing that flexibility is a natural part of a healthy routine.

Weeks Eight and Beyond

1. Is it too soon to move a nine-week-old baby up to a four-hour feeding schedule?

Most likely, yes. Many an eager mom wants to fly through this schedule. They think the faster, the better. There are potential problems with this. First, you should relax and just enjoy your baby through the process. If you move ahead with a four-hour schedule at nine weeks, he may not get sufficient milk. This is especially true if it is your first time breast-feeding. Another concern of moving ahead too quickly in a three- to four-month time span is that your milk supply may become inadequate. We warn moms not to move their newborns too quickly to a four-hour feeding schedule before those babies are sleeping through the night.

2. My baby is three months old. We recently went to visit some relatives for a week and now she's off schedule. How long will it take me to get her back into her regular routine?

Whenever you go on a trip, your baby is bound to get off schedule. It may be due to time zone changes, airports, or grandma's insistence on holding the baby when he should be sleeping. On these occasions, let the relatives enjoy the baby. She will not be a baby for long. Yes, it may take a few days to get her back on schedule when you get home. There may be some crying and protesting from your little one, but in about three days she should be back on track. Again, consider context as you nurture your baby. There may be variables in your daily routine. Remember, your routine should serve you, not shackle you.

During travel you should also consider context. This is especially true if you're on an airplane and your baby begins crying. Some moms think that once the baby starts crying on a plane, they must let her cry herself to sleep before the next feeding. Please consider those around you. Don't adhere to a strict feeding routine at the expense of the passengers around you. This is rigid. Give your baby a bottle or do whatever else you can to stop her from crying during the flight. Place the preciousness of others above your baby's feeding schedule.

Once the routine is broken, either go ahead and feed at her next scheduled time or readjust the schedule to feed in three to four hours. You will not lose ground being flexible when traveling.

3. My twelve-week-old has been sleeping through the night for four weeks, but the last couple of nights he woke up at 3 A.M. What should I do when this happens?

Since your baby has proven he is capable of sleeping through the night, begin by assessing the situation. Is your baby too warm or too cold? Does he have a cold? Did the cat jump into the crib? Use good judgment when deciding what you are going to do. While you may offer a middle-of-the-night feeding, be careful not to create a new pattern of night feeding.

We particularly are concerned for moms who may have several other children plus a newborn. You should slow down with your newborn and realize that you need to be careful about your milk supply. With more children you are far more busy. Due to your busy schedule and possibly an inadequate diet, your milk supply may not be as high in fat content as necessary. Watch your baby's weight gain. You may even decide to supplement your baby at night in order to guarantee he's getting enough nutrition. Remember, the routine is between three to **four** hours for feeding.

4. My breast-fed baby is thirteen weeks old. Is she ready to move to twelve hours of nighttime sleep?

At this age, a breast-fed baby can extend his nighttime sleep to nine to ten hours. The bottle-fed baby can usually go longer. However, breast-feeding mothers must stay mindful of their milk production. Letting your baby sleep longer than nine or ten hours at night may not afford you enough time during the day for sufficient stimulation. Of course, this will not hold true for every mother, but it can happen. Therefore if you're breast-feeding and are concerned about a decrease in your milk supply, do not let your baby sleep more than ten hours at night through this phase.

5. My triplets are four months old by adjusted age. They are feeding every four hours but not sleeping through the night. Why?

Rule one governing nighttime sleep: do not lengthen the time between daytime feedings until your babies are sleeping at least nine to ten hours at night. They need their feedings every three hours during the day. This helps them to distinguish night from day. Also, it assures that all nutritional needs are being met. A basic three-hour routine right now will get your triplets on the right track.

6. My three-month-old has been sleeping through the night for several weeks. Now she is starting to wake up during the night. Why is this happening, and what should I do?

This is fairly typical. Probably she is going through a growth spurt. For the next couple of days, add a feeding or two to her routine. If she is on a $3^{1}/_{2}$- to 4-hour schedule, go back to three hours between feedings for a portion of the daily routine. This situation is temporary. However, look for a reoccurrence at six months. It could also be a prelude to your child's need for additional nutrition. Check with your pediatrician concerning when your baby should start on cereal.

7. My baby is three and a half months old and is not napping well for her third nap. What should I do?

At this age, if your baby is getting a short third nap each day, just make sure the other two are $1^1/2$ to 2 hours long. If she sleeps 30 to 45 minutes for the third nap, that's okay. That is enough to get her through the evening.

8. My baby has been gaining weight just fine, but now at four months he is not gaining at the same rate. Is this cause for concern?

If you are seeing a steady decrease in the rate of weight gain, it may be. It could signal the inception of a serious medical condition or possibly your child is not getting enough food to grow on. While the first condition must be diagnosed by your doctor, the second can be checked by you. First, check your milk supply. If at any time you question its adequacy, you observe routine fussiness after feedings, or your baby is having difficulty going the appropriate duration between feedings, review the external stresses in your life. Eliminate those stressful areas or situations that you can do without. This is true whether baby is four weeks or four months old.

Ask yourself the following: Are you too busy or not getting enough sleep? Are you drinking enough liquids? Is your calorie intake adequate? Are you dieting too soon? Are you following your doctor's recommendation for supplemental vitamins during lactation? If you find your baby is still not content after checking all the external factors, consider the following:

1. Questioning your milk supply in the first two months: For a

baby between three and eight weeks old, consider feeding on a strict 2^1/$_2$ hour routine for five to seven days. If your milk production increases (as demonstrated by the baby becoming more content and sleeping better), work your way back to the three-hour minimum. If no improvement comes, work back to three hours with the aid of a formula complement for the benefit of your baby and your own peace of mind.

2. Questioning your milk supply in the fourth month: The same basic principles apply to this age category. If your baby is between four and six months of age and you question your milk supply, add a couple of feedings to your daytime routine. One of our mothers, also a pediatrician, felt she was losing her milk supply at four months. She did two things. She added a fifth feeding to her day, and she stopped dieting. In less than one week her milk supply was back to normal.

Other mothers found success by returning to a fairly tight three-hour schedule. Once their milk supply returned to normal, they gradually returned to their previous routine. If no improvement comes after five to seven days consider a formula complement. Adding a few extra feedings during the day is not a setback in your parenting, but necessary to ensure a healthy balance between breast-feeding and the related benefits of PDF.

Chapter Eleven

....

Parenting Potpourri:

Topics of Interest to New Parents

*I*f you are a new or prospective parent, you probably are seeking answers to a variety of baby-related questions. In this chapter we address some topics that are likely to be of interest to you; they are arranged in alphabetical order for easy reference. (Much of this material is dealt with more extensively in *On Becoming Babywise II*; there is more information available about *On Becoming Babywise II* at the end of this book.)

Achievement Levels

Much has been written regarding what an infant is supposed to be doing physically during his or her first year of life. This includes mastering such tasks as shaking a rattle, saying "da da," reaching for bright objects, and crawling. There are three important things to remember here. First, a baby's basic routine enhances learning. Order is an ally of the learning process. Second, infants will differ in the age at which they master skills. There is no cause for alarm if your child seems to develop skills more slowly than you believe he or she should, nor should you constantly compare your child's development with your neighbor's child. Third, along with his or her physical development, your baby will become more and more responsive to moral training. Be careful not to focus solely on your baby's physical accomplishments without giving due consideration to his or her developing attitudes. If you have concerns regarding developmental milestones, bring them to your pediatrician's attention.

Baby Blues

Postpartum depression is commonly referred to as "baby blues" and is now receiving significant attention from the media. Physically, there is a hormonal change that takes place in a mother right after delivery. For some women, it takes longer for those hormones to be brought back into balance.

Although some women find themselves depressed and weepy several days after giving birth, not all women experience postpartum depression. Many who do have certain traits in common—they're not on a routine, they nurse frequently, and they are up several times during the night—all of which leave them in a perpetual state of exhaustion. Each of these symptoms can be traced back to the strain that lack of routine puts on a mother. Constant fatigue will do your body no favor. You can greatly minimize the symptoms of postpartum depression by keeping yourself on a good routine, getting plenty of rest, and watching your diet. If you find that after several weeks you are still abnormally melancholy, talk to your obstetrician.

Baby Equipment

One thing to remember about baby equipment is that much of it is optional except for car seats. You don't need to follow all the recommended baby equipment lists that appear in parenting magazines or in baby stores. Your baby isn't going to know or care if he or she has coordinating furniture, so don't worry if the prettiest is not in your budget. There are some items—beyond the usual high chair, stroller, changing table, and crib—that would be helpful and can be borrowed from a friend or relative. Also, you can get great deals at garage sales.

Baby Monitor

A monitor can serve a useful purpose by allowing you to hear your baby if you happen to have a large home or are working outdoors during your baby's nap. Unless baby's room is far away from yours, there is no need to keep it by your bedside at night. You will hear your baby cry during those hours. During the still of the night, the monitor can magnify every sound your baby makes, robbing you of needed sleep. The last thing your child needs in the morning is a cranky parent.

Car Seat

A car seat should be functional not only for your infant but also for your toddler. Think long term when you make this investment. Some car seats are very stylish and work fine for your infant but may not be practical for a growing toddler, thus necessitating the purchase of a second car seat. An infant younger than six months does not have strong neck muscles, so you want to prevent his or her head from rolling from side to side while driving. This can be accomplished by rolling cloth diapers or receiving blankets and using these to support each side of your baby's head, or you can purchase special inserts made for infant car seats that accomplish the same purpose.

Crib

Cribs, cradles, and cots are not products of the industrial revolution as some might guess. They have been used by parents for millennia. For example, three ancient Mediterranean societies (Greek, Roman, and Hebrew) all used cribs for their babies.

The cradle, which is an infant crib with rocking motion, gained popularity in the Middle Ages. Eventually it became a status symbol of wealth. The use of cribs and cradles has not been limited to Europe or the Mediterranean basin. Mothers in primitive settings even today hang cribs from the ceiling of their huts, where they can gently rock their babies as they pass by. For twentieth-century parents, the crib is one of the most basic pieces of baby furniture they will own. Give thought to the one you will buy or borrow. After all, nearly half of your child's existence for the first eighteen months of life will be spent in it.

When deciding on a crib, look for certain features. The mattress should fit snugly against all four sides, and it should be firm and of good quality. A snug fit prevents the baby from getting any of his body parts stuck between the mattress and the slats. The guardrail should be at least twenty-six inches above the top of the mattress. This will discourage any attempt to climb out when the baby is older. The spaces between the crib slats should be no more than 2³/8 inches apart. A crib bumper guard is a good investment and is safer for the baby than using pillows or stuffed animals. The latter should be kept out of the newborn's crib because of the potential danger of suffocation.

The location of the crib in the room is another consideration. Avoid placing the crib near drafty windows, heaters, or hot air ducts. A steady blast of hot air can dry out your baby's nose and throat, leading to respiratory problems.

Infant Seat

You will use the infant seat from day one and use it more than any other piece of equipment in the early weeks and months. When your child is old enough to be spoon fed, an infant seat is preferable to a high chair, since at this age the child does not have the strength to sit up. Please note: The infant seat is not a car seat.

Infant Sling

There is a place and time for backpacks, snuggles, and slings, such as when mom, dad, and their baby are out shopping, hiking, or taking a walk. But it is not a good substitute for the crib. In some third-world nations and primitive settings, mothers carry their babies in an infant sling as they move through their day. We have visited these nations and talked with these mothers. Their actions are not based on a need to create an attachment with their child nor spurred on by Freud's writing. For these mothers it is simply a matter of convenience and safety. Because where they go, the baby must go.

The promotion of the theory that the sling serves as an artificial womb and is necessary to help stabilize a baby's psychological passage into the world has definitely popularized it. This is why the sling is so popular in attachment-parenting circles. In terms of bio-mechanics, carrying a baby in a sling many hours a day may increase neck and back problems or even create them. Like all pieces of equipment, use it thoughtfully. It is not a second womb.

Playpen

Once parents have their infant's eating and sleeping patterns under control, it's time to do the same with waketime activities. This goal is best accomplished by using the playpen, an invaluable piece of equipment. Here are some of the benefits of using a playpen.

1. *It provides a safe environment.* Playpens are a safe environment for an infant when mom's attention must be elsewhere and it's not the baby's naptime. Mom can take a shower or unload the groceries from the car, care for other children, and do a host of other activities knowing her baby is safe.

2. *It doubles as a portable bed.* The playpen can be a portable bed. Especially useful when visiting another home, the playpen gives the baby a clean and familiar place to sleep.

3. *It offers a structured learning center.* Most importantly, your baby's first structured learning takes place in the playpen. The partnership a child has with the playpen helps establish foundational intellectual skills.

Planned daily playpen times allow a little one the opportunity to develop:

a) Mental focusing skills (the ability to concentrate on an object or activity at hand and not be constantly distracted)

b) A sustained attention span

c) Creativity (Creativity is the product of boundaries, not freedom. With absolute freedom, there is no need for creative thinking or problem solving.)

d) The ability to entertain himself or herself

e) Orderliness

Parents can begin using the playpen as a safe environment or as a portable bed soon after the baby is born. Playpen time (using the playpen as a learning center) may begin as soon as the baby has alert waketimes of fifteen to thirty minutes. At least one of those waketimes each day can be spent in the playpen. By two months of age, the playpen should be a well-established part of your baby's routine.

Start by putting your baby in the playpen for fifteen minutes once or twice a day. Select times when the baby is fresh and alert (not right before naptime). Put several interesting toys within your baby's reach, or use a crib gym or a mobile. Local libraries carry books that will describe the types of toys or activities your baby is likely to be interested in at each stage of development.

Bathing Your Baby

Your baby should not receive his or her first full bath at home until the remainder of the umbilical cord has fallen off (seven to fourteen days after birth). Never interfere with the natural process of the cord falling off. After it does, you are free to bathe your baby in either a baby tub or on a towel placed in the kitchen sink.

Always monitor the water temperature; it should be warm to the touch. An infant doesn't need to receive a full bath every day—a sponge bath some days is sufficient. Soap doesn't need to be used every day either; overuse may dry your baby's skin. The most important bath-related advice we can give you is this: never leave your baby alone in water. Adhering to this rule without fail can prevent tragedy.

Bonding with Your Baby

The concept of parent-child bonding, once a precise academic theory, has evolved into one of general application to the parent-child relationship. The theory concerns itself with ensuring that a new mother does not reject her offspring. How is this achieved? It is asserted that the first minutes or hours after birth constitute a sensitive period during which a mother should have close physical contact with her newborn. This theory supposes that a mother would instinctively be drawn closer to her child in the future if bonding (brought about by face-to-face and skin-to-skin contact) takes place soon after birth. This supposedly gives an advantage to the child and will help him or her reach optimal potential. If only parenthood were that easy!

While maternal-infant bonding is an interesting psychological idea, research has not substantiated in human beings the cause-and-effect relationship this theory speaks of. And although nonrational animals show some instinctive tendency of this sort, speculating that rational man responds similarly is scientifically unacceptable. Anthropology—the study of mankind—is very different from zoology, the study of animals.[1]

There is nothing wrong with a newborn cuddling with his or her mother right after birth or having a close time together with his or her new family. If it's possible, we encourage you to do that. Take time to acknowledge the wonderful creation of a new life. But don't think those first minutes are more binding or important than all the hours and days that will follow. Building a healthy parent-child relationship doesn't take place in a moment of time; it's a long-term process. Your baby will not be permanently impaired if there is a lack of physical contact with mom right after birth.[2]

Cesarean Birth

The purpose for cesarean section surgery is basic: to safeguard the life of the baby or the mother. Most often referred to as a c-section, delivery is accomplished through an incision in the abdominal wall and uterus. The decision to do a c-section may be made either prior to your due date because of a known condition or because of an unexpected complication during labor. In either case, competent doctors have your best interests in mind.

More unnecessary c-sections are performed today than in years past. There are two primary reasons for this fact. First, we have developed greater technology for saving babies. Second, there are more lawsuits against obstetricians and gynecologists today, forcing them to exercise conservative, lower-risk treatment. Keep in mind that having a c-section performed is a medical decision that in no way reflects on your motherhood. There is no need to feel guilty or embarrassed over it. Just be thankful you and your baby are healthy.

Church Nurseries and Baby-Sitters

Nursery workers and baby-sitters provide a wonderful service. Unfortunately, some moms and dads demand that the nursery workers keep their babies on a rigid routine. Parents should be gracious and appreciative when leaving a child in the nursery or in other special baby-sitting situations. Nursery workers cannot be obligated to maintain your baby's schedule because there is no way they can keep track of ten, fifteen, or twenty different schedules.

When your baby goes to the nursery, leave a bottle of water, formula, or breast milk and give the nursery worker the freedom to do what he or she thinks is best. It won't harm your baby's routine to be fed earlier than what is scheduled at this time. You will be able to return to your baby's normal routine later in the day.

We are encouraged by the fact that so many parents understand the value of order in their lives and their children's lives. But sometimes people redefine order to mean rigidity, and that leads to imbalance. Balance includes both structure and flexibility.

Circumcision

Circumcision is almost as old as history itself. The practice was historically (though not exclusively) a Jewish rite. Today, medical experts and studies tend to affirm that there are some modest benefits to circumcision, although not all agree on the necessity of it. Evidence suggests that circumcision may decrease the risk of urinary tract infection and that it virtually eliminates the possibility of cancer of the penis. Parents should also consider the social ramifications of circumcision. How will your son feel in a locker room full of other boys during his school years?

For the infant, circumcision is not the traumatic experience that some portray. His minor surgery and any discomfort felt will not be rooted in his memory any more than will his being pricked with a heel stick during his PKU blood test soon after birth.

Crib Death

The unexpected death of a seemingly healthy baby is referred to as Sudden Infant Death Syndrome (SIDS) or crib death. What do we know about SIDS? We know it's responsible for seven thousand deaths a year and is neither predictable nor preventable. There are more male victims, especially among those who are born prematurely, and it occurs more often among babies of minorities, young single mothers, and those who smoke.

A child can be victimized by SIDS any time during the first year, with the highest percentage of these deaths occurring between the second and fourth months. More babies die of SIDS in the winter months than in summer, and more in colder climates than in warmer ones.

Some family-bed advocates suggest that sleeping with your baby can decrease the possibility of SIDS. This conclusion is drawn from data compiled in third-world nations, where fewer SIDS cases were reported among children who slept with their parents compared to SIDS cases in North America. Their conclusion ignores some very important information which we need to share with you. First, most third-world nations are found in warmer climates where SIDS frequency would be expected to be four to five times less due to the absence of cold weather. And second, when a comparison is made within a third-world society, families whose parents sleep with their children have equal or higher rates of infant deaths than those who don't sleep with their children.

Does bed-sharing with your infant really reduce the possibility of SIDS? The American Academy of Pediatrics says no to that question. The AAP in collaboration with a National Institute of Child Health and Human Development subcommittee concluded there was no evidence that shared sleep reduces the risk of Sudden Infant Death Syndrome and indeed, it may increase the risk.[3]

Today research strongly suggests and the American Academy of Pediatrics recommends that putting a baby on his or her back for sleep, rather than on the baby's tummy, reduces the risk of SIDS.[4] What is not conclusive is whether back sleeping is the primary or secondary factor in the reduction of risk. Does the supine position (wholly on the back) remove the child from soft surfaces and gas-trapping objects (mattresses, pillows, crib liners), which could be the actual risk factor, or is it actually the biomechanics of tummy-sleeping? More research is needed to answer that question. Meanwhile, we suggest you speak to your health care provider if you have any questions concerning SIDS and the positioning of your baby. Parents ask us if back positioning will interfer with the establishment of healthy sleep? The answer is no.

One last word about crib death. The one thing that most pediatricians agree upon is the need for a firm mattress of good quality. Soft mattresses with questionable stuffing material should be avoided. Spend the extra money required for a good mattress.

Diapers

As new parents, you have a choice between disposable or cloth diapers. It really is a matter of personal preference. As a general rule, you will change your baby's diaper at each feeding. PDF babies average six to eight diaper changes a day coinciding with their feedings.

At the nighttime feeding it may not be necessary to change your baby's diaper unless it is soaked or soiled. Remember, your goal is for your baby to sleep through the night, not to wake up for a diaper change. When your baby begins to sleep through the night, use a medium size disposable diaper or two cloth diapers. They will seem larger only because today's babies are not expected to sleep through the night as early as those on PDF.

Diaper Rash

A diaper rash may be caused by yeast infections, food allergies, new teeth, or sitting too long in a messy diaper. If your baby has sensitive skin, he or she may be more prone to diaper rash. Have your pediatrician recommend an over-the-counter medication for minor irritations or a prescription medication for more severe problems.

Grandparents

There is a special relationship between the third generation and the first. Within reason, you will want to take advantage of every opportunity for grandparents to enjoy your child. However, don't assume your parents want to baby-sit or abuse their generous offers to do so.

And don't surrender your parenting responsibilities to your parents. While they may very much enjoy their grandchildren, they are not the parents—you are.

Many grandparents travel a great distance to visit soon after the baby is born. That visit can either be a blessing or a problem, depending on your relationship and just how like-minded you are. You may want to ask the traveling grandparents to visit ten days to two weeks after the baby is born. By then you will have worked through your basic parenting approach and will feel somewhat comfortable with what you are doing. Having a high-powered, take-charge relative come in right after birth can be very hard on a new mother's emotions. A husband can help by protecting his wife from unwelcome intrusions. We would strongly suggest that you provide each set of grandparents with their own copy of *On Becoming Babywise*. Life is much easier when the grandparents know what you are doing and why you are doing it.

Growth Spurts

Growth spurts are just that—spurts of growth that come on your baby. The first may come as early as the tenth day preceded with a sleepy day and voracious breast-feeding. They may show up again at three, six, and twelve weeks, and then again at four and six months. If your baby has been content after feedings but suddenly no longer is, he or she probably is beginning a growth spurt. The nursing mom may find the baby wanting to nurse longer, and there will be some frustration on baby's part if the mother doesn't have enough milk. If you are breast-feeding, these spurts may necessitate some extra feedings for a couple of days to increase your milk supply to meet your baby's increased demand. If you are feeding approximately every 3 hours when this happens, drop back to 2¹/2 for a couple of times a day. If you are bottle-feeding and suspect your baby is experiencing a growth spurt, simply offer more formula per feeding.

Immunizations

The ability to protect our children from the tragedies of polio and other deadly diseases is one of the blessings of our day. Medical research has provided us with effective immunizations that build up antibodies to fight off invading disease. But the vaccines are useless if the child never receives them. Parents are responsible to see that their child is fully protected. The eight common vaccinations offered are polio, diphtheria, pertussis (whooping cough), tetanus, rubella (German measles), mumps, measles, hepatitis, and *Haemophilus influenza,* type b (Hib). Most pediatricians start routine immunizations within the first two months. Because immunization schedules change frequently as better vaccines and more information become available, you will need to ask your pediatrician for a current time table of vaccinations. If you have concerns or questions about any of them, by all means, ask your pediatrician.

The Microwave and the Bottle

Occasionally you may want to heat your baby's bottle in a microwave oven. That can be dangerous unless certain precautions are taken. Microwaves heat foods unevenly, so be sure to shake the bottle well after heating and squirt a dab of milk on your wrist to test for warmth. Unlike formula, breast milk can be destroyed in the heating process if care is not taken. When heating your baby's bottle, be sure to loosen the top to allow for heat expansion; otherwise it may explode.

Nursing Twins

For a mother to nurse twins successfully, the PDF plan is a must. Assign a breast to each twin and keep them nursing that specified breast throughout all feedings. This will help the supply to keep up with the unique demand of each twin. Let one twin set the pace, and keep them both on that schedule. If this means you must wake one, do so.

During the first few weeks postpartum, you can nurse your twins simultaneously using a football hold—your arms are bent to support the back of each baby while each head rests on a breast. As they grow, your babies will have to nurse one at a time. Beyond that distinction, you will be able to implement all other aspects of the parent-directed feeding plan, including feeding routines and sleeping through the night. May you thoroughly enjoy your "double portion"! (For a more complete discussion of how to deal with a multiple birth, see chapter 9, "Multiple Birth: The Endless Party.")

Pacifiers and Thumb-Sucking

Breast-feeding mothers hoping to establish healthy feed/wake/sleep cycles should not let themselves be used as pacifiers. Some infants have a need to suck a little longer after feeding time. An actual pacifier is very useful for them. That is especially true of infants who nurse so efficiently that feeding time lasts a total of only five to ten minutes. Pacifiers can also be used to extend the time between feedings when a baby is fussy but not hungry. However, be careful not to use the pacifier as a "plug" whenever your baby fusses, nor should it become a sleep prop. Don't create habits that will have to be broken later.

Some children will not take a pacifier but find their thumb instead. That's fine. Consider how long you will use the pacifier or allow your child to suck his or her thumb. If thumb-sucking persists past two years, limit it to the child's bedroom. That boundary will help you eliminate the practice later on.

Sleeping with Your Baby (The Family Bed)

It is common for children in third-world countries to sleep in the same bed with their parents. In most cases this is done for pragmatic reasons: there is only one bed and often only one room. Poverty forces the sleeping arrangement, not the pursuit of psychological health for the child. For modern America, the family bed finds its roots in the birth-trauma theory. As stated previously, the practice allows for the constant presence of the mother, as required by the theory's hypothesis.

The family bed is unsafe. As stated in chapter 3 and earlier in this chapter, the American Academy of Pediatrics public policy statement warns that bed sharing might actually increase the risk of SIDS. The Consumer Protection Safety Commission warns parents against sleeping with their infants because of the death hazard. They are joined by the vast majority of health care professionals in America who agree the practice is dangerous.

Authorities in Madison County, Illinois, are warning parents not to sleep with their infants. According to coroner Dallas Burke, five roll-over deaths occurred in the first eight months of 1997.[5] Multiply what is happening in Madison County across the country and you will begin to understand why so many medical experts are shouting warnings about the dangers of attachment parenting with its over-emphasis on infant cosleeping.

One of the most recent cautions against cosleeping comes from Dr. Clifford Nelson, a Multnomah County, Oregon, deputy medical examiner. In an article posted on the Internet, September 1996, titled "Co-Sleeping Deaths," he notes, "The following unfortunate story is reported hundreds of times in the United States each year."

In a recent case a thirteen-day-old female infant was found dead between her mother and father. "The baby was last breast-fed by her mother at 2:00 A.M., at which time she was brought from her crib into the parents' bed. The exhausted mother had decided to keep the baby in bed with her in case she awoke again needing to be fed," said Nelson. Nelson goes on to observe: "The social consequences of these cases [such as the thirteen-day-old infant suffocation] are far reaching."

Unfortunately, cosleeping suffocations have become more difficult to discern in recent years as more and more infant deaths have been labeled as "SIDS" cases. Without a thorough autopsy, it is virtually impossible for a medical examiner or coroner to distinguish between an actual SIDS death and an infant suffocation death. Yet, as Dr. Nelson pointed out, actual infant suffocations are in the *hundreds* to *thousands* a year.

In addition to the potential for infant suffocation, there are other not-so-obvious difficulties with infant or child cosleeping. According to Dr. Sandra Kaplan, associate chairman of the Department of Psychiatry for Child and Adolescent Psychiatry at a hospital in New York, separate beds for children "build a sense of competence." She says the family bed can be "used as a contraceptive by parents who should, instead, be dealing with the issue between them in other ways."[6]

Dr. Laura Popper, a pediatrician and professor of clinical pediatrics at Mt. Sinai Medical Hospital, views the family bed as "dangerous," and has found it is used by "the more insecure mothers." And Dr. Richard Ferber, director of the Center for Pediatric Sleep Disorders at Children's Hospital, Boston, notes, "It's well documented that the more people there are in a bed, the less soundly parents will sleep."

Some countries discourage the practice. New Zealand, for example, has cut down on infant death dramatically by educating young parents to the dangers of sleeping with a baby. As more infant deaths are reported in America, state legislators are beginning to consider laws designed to discourage the practice. Why take a chance?

Sleeping with your baby creates needs but doesn't fulfill them. Your child won't be any more secure, feel more loved, or have any greater advantages in life than a child who sleeps alone. What the nighttime parenting advocates gloss over are sleep problems created as the child grows older.

We believe this practice hinders the development of trust between parent and child, since the child is never given the opportunity to learn how to trust. The child who can sleep alone, knowing that mom and dad will come when needed, is much more secure than the child who is never alone and can't exist outside his or her parents' presence. With the latter, trust is based upon proximity rather than a relationship. The measure of a child's security is never found in the presence of his or her parent, but in how well the child copes away from parents. The benefits of shared sleep are clearly exaggerated.

Shared sleep confuses infant sleep cycles. And separation anxiety often occurs when the child is asked to leave mom and dad's bed. If an infant is placed in his or her own bed and room right from the beginning, no separation anxiety takes place since no dependent nighttime relationship is established. Also, shared sleep has proven problematic for many nursing mothers since the fear of rolling on top of the baby creates anxiety which affects sleep and milk production.

Contrast the nighttime peace associated with a baby sleeping soundly in his or her crib to the squeezed, squirming, and disrupted sleep moms and dads who share a bed with their baby experience. As one mother states, in reference to having her baby sleep with her and her husband, "It wasn't as natural as they said it would be. Every sound, move, and restless fit the child made was amplified. We held our breath hoping upon hope that the child would not wake and demand of me. My comfort during the day and night became a reluctant duty and not a true expression of a mother's love. The theory robbed me of the joy of motherhood."

There is nothing wrong with a child taking a nap with mom or dad once in a while or with cuddling the baby in bed before everyone gets up. But patterns you establish in the first couple of days, weeks, and months, whether right or wrong, will become those to which your little one will adjust. The longer wrong patterns persist, the harder they will be to break.

The child could smother beneath a sleeping adult, become wedged between the mattress or against an adjacent wall, or suffocate face down, especially on a water bed. These terrible things do happen. There is not a single benefit gained that can possibly outweigh the risk.

Spitting Up

This is a common event in the life of every infant. At first it may be frightening to a new parent, but it is normal and not a cause for alarm. Proper burping during and after feeding can minimize and sometimes eliminate the problem. (For a discussion of how to burp your baby, see the material near the end of chapter 4 headed "Burping Your Baby.") Your baby may have taken in more milk than he or she needed. Refeeding is not usually necessary. Keep in mind that babies vary tremendously; some rarely spit up, while others spit up all the time. If your child is growing, gaining weight, and is happy and healthy, then he or she is fine.

Projectile vomiting is not the same thing as spitting up. Instead of bringing back up just part of his or her meal, the baby powerfully ejects the entire contents of the stomach. If your baby experiences this type of vomiting frequently, call your pediatrician.

Starting Solid Foods

Parent-directed feeding continues with the addition of solids (baby food and table foods) to your baby's menu. Add solids at existing family mealtimes, working toward three meals a day. With the production of saliva at about three months of age, you will see the baby preparing for a change in menu (although you will not begin feeding your child solids until he or she is four to six months of age).

In your child's first year, the calories he or she gains from liquids (breast milk or formula) are of primary importance. During the second half of the first year, a gradual transition occurs. Though your baby may still drink as much at twelve months as at six months, he or she will need more and more calories from solids.

Generally, you should start adding solids to your baby's diet at between four and six months depending on the baby's weight gain and sleep patterns. Your pediatrician will advise you. The first food to add to your baby's meals is rice cereal. Later, you will add other single-grain cereals. Specific information about adding solids to your baby's diet are discussed in *On Becoming Babywise II*.

Teething

When a tooth begins to break through the gum, a baby experiences the condition commonly referred to as teething. Like jaundice, teething isn't a disease; it's a condition of growth. Your baby's first teeth will push through at between six and eight months of age. By six months, one baby out of three has one tooth, and by nine months, the typical baby has three teeth. The natural process of teething should not interfere with breast-feeding, since the sucking is done by the tongue and palate, not by the gums.

Irritability, fussiness, increased salivation, and a slightly raised temperature sometimes accompany new teeth. As uncomfortable as these symptoms may be, teething is not a catchall excuse for chronic poor behavior or a drastic change in your baby's routine.

Weaning Your Baby

Weaning, by today's definition, is the process by which parents offer food supplements in place of, or in addition to, mother's milk. That process begins the moment parents offer a bottle of formula or when their baby first tastes cereal. From that moment on, weaning is generally a gradual process.

From the Breast

The duration of breast-feeding has varied from the extremes of birth to fifteen years. No one can say for sure at what age weaning should take place. For some it may be six months, for others a year. Breast-feeding for more than a year is a matter of preference, since adequate supplementary food is usually available. Several thousand years ago, weaning took place at between eighteen and twenty-four months of age. A baby being nursed as long as three years was rare.

At birth, infants are totally dependent on their caregiver to meet their physical needs. But they must gradually become more independent, in small increments. One step toward independence for your baby is the ability to feed himself or herself. You can start the weaning process by eliminating one feeding at a time, going three to four days before dropping the next one. That time frame allows your body to make the proper adjustments in milk reduction.

Usually the late-afternoon feeding is the easiest one to drop, since it is a busy time of day. Replace each feeding with six to eight ounces of formula or milk (depending on the child's age). Pediatricians generally recommend that parents not give their babies cow's milk until they are at least one year of age. If your baby is nine months or older, consider going straight to a cup rather than to a bottle. The transition will be easiest if you have introduced the cup prior to weaning.

From the Bottle

When your baby is one year of age, you can begin to wean him or her from the bottle. Some mothers wean straight to a cup with great success. Although an infant can become very attached to a bottle, you can minimize that problem by not letting your child hold it for extended periods of time. There is a difference between playing with the bottle and drinking from it. The weaning process takes time, so be prepared to be patient. Begin by eliminating the bottle at one meal, then at another, and so on.

Chapter Twelve

Principles for Starting Late

Unfortunately, not all parents start out with the advantages provided by the *Babywise* infant-management plan. Many awaken to the need after their babies are six, twelve, or eighteen months old and still are not sleeping through the night. Is it too late for these parents? Absolutely not. If you are in this situation and desire to correct the problem, the change must begin with you.

Below are some rules and guidelines that will help your baby establish continuous nighttime sleep.

General Rules

1. Make sure you have read and understand the entire contents of this book before proceeding any further.

2. Don't try to make any changes while out-of-town guests or relatives are visiting. You don't need the added pressure of explaining everything you are doing.

3. Start the process of change when your baby is healthy.

General Guidelines

1. Work on your baby's daytime routine for the first four to five days. Keep in mind the three activities you must include and their order—feeding time, waketime, then naptime. Review chapter 6, "Establishing Your Baby's Routine," to determine how many feedings are appropriate in a 24-hour period, given your child's age. For example, at three months of age your baby should be receiving four to five feedings a day. If he or she is six months old, your baby should be receiving three meals a day with a nursing period or a bottle just before bed. If you have been in the habit of rocking or nursing your baby to sleep at naptime, now is the time to eliminate that practice.

2. Review chapter 8, "When Your Baby Cries," and be prepared for some crying. You are moving from a high-comfort style of sleep manipulation to basic training in sleep skills. Initially your baby will not like this change, but it is necessary. In moments of parental stress, be comforted in knowing your baby won't feel abandoned because you have decided that the best thing for him is learning how to fall asleep on his own. Continue to think about and look toward the long-term benefits. Your proactive response is best for the baby and for the entire family.

3. Don't feel the necessity to check on your baby every five minutes while he or she is crying. If you go into your baby's room, try to do so without being seen. If necessary, move the crib so you can see the baby but the baby can't see you. If you feel you must soothe the child, go in briefly and pat him or her on the back. With a soft voice, say, "It's all right," then quietly leave. As a result, your baby will do one of two things: be comforted and fall asleep or roar even louder.

If your baby chooses the latter, don't be discouraged! The crying only means he or she has not yet developed the ability to settle himself or herself. That goal is precisely what you are working toward.

4. Be patient and consistent. For some parents, success comes after one night; for others, it comes after two weeks. The norm, however, is three to five days.

Summary

Retraining is always more difficult than training correctly from the start, but it needs to be done. Parents who love their babies give them what they need; young children need a good night's sleep.

Moms who have made the transition from sleepless nights to peaceful sleep report that their children not only gain the advantage of continuous nighttime sleep, but their daytime disposition also changes. They appear happier, more content, and definitely more manageable. We trust this will be the case with your baby.

We wish you and your family the best as you work at helping your child gain this fundamental skill—the ability to sleep, uninterrupted, right on through the night.

Notes

Chapter Two

1. Dr. Rupert Rogers wrote on the problems of breast-feeding during the 1930s and 1940s. He told mothers to be old-fashioned. What did he mean by that? He said to go back to nursing periods arranged as follows: 6:00 A.M., 9:00 A.M., noon, 3:00 P.M., 6:00 P.M., 10:00 P.M., and once when the baby wakes in the night. Although that type of feeding was a schedule, it wasn't referred to as such. The term "schedule" referred to a nursing technique more than a routine. *Mother's Encyclopedia* (New York: The Parents Institute, Inc., 1951), p. 122.

2. See recommendations by William Sears, M.D., & Martha Sears, R.N., *The Baby Book* (Boston: Little, Brown & Company, 1993), p. 136.

3. William Sears, M.D., & Martha Sears, R.N., *The Baby Book* (Boston: Little, Brown & Company, 1993), p. 343.

4. We don't take issue with a mother who chooses to breast-feed longer than a year because she enjoys that special time. We take issue with the suggestion that the child has a psychological need inherent at birth and if not allowed access to his or her mother's breast, the child's future emotional health is put at risk.

Chapter Three

1. This conclusion was drawn from a study based on thirty-two mother-infant pairs observed over two years. Sixteen families were from the La Leche League, and the other sixteen were not. "Sleep-Wake Patterns of Breast-Fed Infants in the First Two Years of Life," *Pediatrics* 77, no. 3, (March 1986): p. 328.

2. Marc Weissbluth, *Healthy Sleep Habits, Happy Child* (New York, Ballantine Books 1987), p. 44.

3. Ibid., p. 6.

4. American Academy of Pediatrics, "Does Bed Sharing Affect the Risk of SIDS?" *Pediatrics* 100, no. 2 (August 1997): p. 727.

5. An article published in *The Brown University Child Behavior and Development Letter* (Aug 1990), discussed sleep problems encountered by children who slept with their parents.

Chapter Four

1. A baby's immune system is developed by two means. During pregnancy, disease-fighting proteins called antibodies pass from the mother's blood to the baby's blood. They provide temporary protection against the many illnesses to which the mother has been exposed. After birth, the baby's immune system is enhanced with breast milk. That is done two ways: 1) by the passing of the mother's antibodies through the milk, which are then absorbed into the child's bloodstream; and 2) by way of the bifidus factor. Infants are born with millions of tiny organisms in a semidormant state which are members of the lactobacillus-bifidus family. Their growth is stimulated by certain elements in the mother's milk. As these organisms grow, they produce acetic and lactic acids that prevent the growth of many disease-producing organisms, such as E. coli and dysentery bacilli. This does not mean that bottle-fed babies have no immune system; they do, but it is not as protective.

2. *Pediatrics,* 100, no. 6 (December 1997): p. 1036.

3. Ibid., p. 1036.

4. Ibid., pp. 136–137.

5. On January 20, 1995, ABC's *20/20* aired a story dealing with demand-fed, dehydrated infants. This piece showed the American public a child with an amputated leg. The leg was taken because gangrene had set in due to the lack of proper assessment of the real need—adequate nutrition. The mother was feeding on demand but the child wasn't demanding enough.

ABC is not the only major media source that voiced concern. In a front page article in *The Wall Street Journal* on July 22, 1994, reporter Kevin Helliker told the story of an infant who by the end of the first week had taken in so little food that he suffered irreversible brain damage. The mother kept trying to nurse her newborn on demand, despite initial difficulties. Other cases were documented, including two that resulted in death as a result of mothers not recognizing the signs of inadequate milk production.

Similar reports appeared in *Time* on August 22, 1994, *U.S. News & World Report* on December 5, 1994, and on the television news magazine *Primetime Live,* August 4, 1994. According to *The Wall Street Journal,* nearly 200,000 infants a year are diagnosed with "failure to thrive"—most of which are associated with "just feed more often" advice.

6. See the work of Nancy Butte, Cathy Wills, Cynthia Jean, E. O'Brian Smith and Cutberto Garza, "Feeding patterns of exclusively breast-fed infants during the first four months of life," (Houston: USDA/ARS Children's Nutrition Research Center, 1985).

7. Jan Riordan and Kathleen Auerbach, *Breastfeeding and Human Lactation* (Sudbury Mass.: Jones and Bartlett Publishers, 1993), p. 520.

8. Sources supporting these recommended number of feeding times: *American Academy of Pediatrics Policy Statement Pediatrics* 100, no. 6, (December 1997): 1037. Frank Oski, M.D., *Principles and Practice of Pediatrics*, 2nd ed. (Philadelphia: J.B. Lippincott Company, 1994), p. 307; Richard E. Behrman, M.D., Victor C. Vaughan, M.D., Waldo E. Nelson, M.D., *Nelsons Textbook of Pediatrics*, 13th ed. (Philadelphia: W.B. Sauders Company, 1987), p. 124. Kathleen Huggins, *The Nursing Mother's Companion*, 3rd ed. (Boston: The Harvard Common Press, 1995), p. 35. Jan Riordan and Kathleen Auerbach, *Breastfeeding and Human Lactation*, (Sudbury, MA.: Jones and Bartlett Publishers, 1993), pp. 188, 189, 246.

9. Breast-feeding mothers are sometimes warned not to use a bottle. The concern is over "nipple confusion." The belief is that a baby will become confused and refuse the breast if offered a bottle. Although under normal circumstances there will be no need to introduce a bottle to the breast-fed infant in the first few weeks, there will come a time when the bottle will be a welcome friend. After the first few days of breast-feeding, supplementing by bottle rarely causes "nipple confusion." Kathleen Huggins, *The Nursing Mother's Companion*, 3rd ed. (Boston: Harvard Common Press, 1995), p. 73.

Chapter Five

1. The BMI index is derived by dividing the weight expressed in kilograms, by the length (height), expressed in meters squared. The rational for using BMI was an attempt to obtain a more uniform basis of comparison than a simple linear contrast. Using absolute body weight alone as a comparative tool suffers from the fact that it does not embody any reference to the stature of the baby. However, an analysis using BMI allows for a more meaningful comparative study of babies with different birth weights and statures.

Chapter Six

1. Nancy Butte, Cathy Wills, Cynthia Jean, E. O'Brian Smith and Cutberto Garza, "Feeding patterns of exclusively breast-fed infants during the first four months of life." (Houston: USDA/ARS Children's Nutrition Research Center, 1985), p. 298.

Chapter Eight

1. Do the premises we present represent theory or reality? It was with great interest and pleasure that we read the cover story of *Time* magazine, "The E.Q. Factor," (Nancy Gibbs, October 2, 1995, p. 60). The article spotlighted the work of Harvard University professor Daniel Goleman. In his book *Emotional Intelligence* (Bantam Books), Dr. Goleman presents some very interesting findings: children who gain the mastery of delayed gratification learn the virtue of self-control, and hence have a much better life. Children trained in immediate gratification suffer and are left behind.

His study began with a marshmallow and involved a test developed by Dr. Walter Mischel of Columbia University. One at a time, children were brought to a room and offered a marshmallow. They were told they could eat the marshmallow "right now" or if they waited until the researcher got back from running an errand, he would give them a second marshmallow. But they had to wait and not eat the first one. When the test was completed, researchers followed these children as they grew up. This is what they found:

By the time the children reached high school, the children's parents and teachers found that those who, as four-year-olds, had the fortitude to hold out for the second marshmallow generally grew up to be better adjusted and more popular, adventurous, confident, and dependable teenagers. The children who were raised with immediate gratification training, who could not wait for the greater benefits, were more likely to be lonely, easily frustrated, and stubborn. They buckled under stress and shied away from challenges. When comparing their scores on the Scholastic Aptitude Test, the kids who waited for the second marshmallow scored on average 206 points higher. Dr. Goleman's conclusion: "It seems that the ability to delay gratification is a master skill, a triumph of the reasoning brain over the impulsive one."

We spoke by phone with Dr. Walter Mischel of Columbia University to ascertain the length of time the children waited between marshmallows. He told us that the original study used a delayed gratification factor of fifteen minutes. We then repeated the test with twenty-five children, ages three, four, and five, all former PDF babies who developed healthy sleep habits. For our three-year-olds, we set the gratification factor at ten minutes. But we extended Dr. Mischel's time by five minutes for the four- and five-year-olds, making the children wait twenty minutes. This is what we found:

- Of the 5 three-year-olds tested: all waited for the second marshmallow.
- Of the 15 four-year-olds tested: all waited for the second marshmallow.
- Of the 5 five-year-olds tested: all waited for the second marshmallow.

Dr. Goleman's research focused on the result of delayed gratification, but not on the method of achievement. Yet obviously all the children we studied demonstrated a conscious choice for delayed gratification for the greater gain. Could something as basic as an infant feeding routine, healthy naps, continuous nighttime sleep, definite boundaries, and a healthy dose of "otherness" training be the channel for success? We believe so.

Chapter Eleven

1. Michael E. Lamb, Ph.D., from the Department of Pediatrics at the University of Utah Medical School, summarizes our position: "The preponderance of the evidence thus suggests that extended contact [the bonding theory] has no clear effects on maternal behavior." Michael E. Lamb, Ph.D., in *Pediatrics,* 70, no. 5 (November 1982), p. 768.

2. For an excellent challenge to the myth of bonding please see Diane Eyer, *Mother Infant-Bonding: Scientific Fiction,* (New Haven: Yale University Press. 1992).

3. *Pediatrics* (August 1997), p. 272.

4. National Institute of Child Health and Human Development, "Sudden Infant Death Syndrome," April 1997.

5. *The Hawk Eye* (August 28, 1997).

6. "The Family Bed: Sleeping with the Young & the Restless," *Forward* (Aug. 9, 1996).

Subject Index

Healthy Baby

Growth Charts

SIGNS OF ADEQUATE NUTRITION
Chart One—Week One

If you're breast-feeding, monitoring your baby's growth is of vital concern. How do you know if your baby is getting enough food to grow on? There are a number of objective indicators to healthy growth and proper nutrition. Indicators of healthy baby growth provide mom guidance and feedback as to how well she and her baby are doing. The following indicators represent healthy signs of growth during the first week of life.

1. Your baby goes to the breast and nurses.
2. Your baby is nursing a minimum of eight times in a 24-hour period.
3. Your baby is nursing over fifteen minutes at each nursing period.
4. You can hear your baby swallowing milk.
5. Your baby has passed his first stool called meconium. (Make sure you let the nurses know that you are tracking your baby's growth indicators.)
6. Your baby's stooling pattern progresses from meconium (greenish black) to brownie batter transition stools, to yellow stools by the fourth or fifth day. This is one of the most positive signs that your baby is getting enough milk.
7. Within 24 to 48 hours, your baby starts having wet diapers, (increasing to two or three a day.) By the end of the first week wet diapers are becoming more frequent.

Unhealthy growth indicators for the first week.

1. Your baby is not showing any desire to nurse or has a very weak suck.
2. Your baby fails to nurse eight times in a 24-hour period.
3. Your baby tires quickly at the breast and cannot sustain at least fifteen minutes of nursing.
4. Your baby continually falls asleep at the breast before taking a full feeding.
5. You hear a clicking sound accompanied by dimpled checks while baby is nursing.
6. Your baby's stooling pattern is not progressing to yellow stools within a week's time.
7. Your baby has not had wet any diapers within 48 hours of birth.

Using the chart to keep track of your baby's vital health indicators can make the difference between healthy and unhealthy growth. If you wish, make a copy of the chart and place it in a convenient location (on a refrigerator, above the crib, etc.). Place the appropriate ($\sqrt{}$) mark or letter designated for each occurrence. For example, if your baby nurses nine times on day two, then place nine checks on that day. If your baby passes his first meconium stool on the second day, then place an "M" on that day. Knowing what to expect and measuring results will get you and your baby off to a great start.

HEALTHY BABY GROWTH CHART: Chart One Week 1

Birth Weight _____ lb. /oz. Birth Length _____ inches

HEALTH GROWTH INDICATORS	DAY 1	DAY 2	DAY 3	DAY 4	DAY 5	DAY 6	DAY 7
Place a check (✔) for each feeding in a 24 hour period. (Minimum of 8 feedings a day.)							
Place a check (✔) for each nursing period of 15 or more minutes in length.							
Place a "M" for the first stool (Meconium) and a "T" for each brownie battered transition stool.							
Place a "Y" to record each yellow stool. (Milk stools should appear by the 4th or 5th day.)							
Place a check (✔) for each wet diaper. (Wet diapers should start to appear by 48 hours or sooner.)							

7–10 days: Weight _____ lb. /oz. Length _____ inches

Any two consecutive days of deviation from what is listed as normal *should be reported immediately to your pediatrician.*

© Gary Ezzo & Robert Bucknam

SIGNS OF ADEQUATE NUTRITION

Chart Two—Weeks Two through Four

Just because things have gone well in the first week does not mean you can slack off from monitoring your baby's healthy growth signs. After the first week, some of the healthy growth indicators begin to change. This chart represents healthy baby growth indicators to be monitored over the next three weeks. Please note the changes.

Here is the checklist for the next three weeks.

1. Your baby is nursing at least eight times a day.

2. Your baby over the next three weeks has two to five or more yellow stools daily. (This number will probably decrease after the first month.)

3. Your baby during this period should start to have six to eight wet diapers a day, some saturated.

4. Your baby's urine is clear, not yellow.

5. Your baby has a strong suck, you see milk, and you can hear an audible swallow.

6. You're noticing increased signs of alertness during your baby's waketime.

7. Your baby is gaining weight and growing in length.

Unhealthy growth indicators are:

1. Your baby is not getting eight feedings a day.

2. Your baby in the first month has small, scant, and infrequent stools.

3. Your baby does not have the appropriate number of wet diapers given his age.

4. Your baby's urine is concentrated and bright yellow.

5. Your baby has a weak or tiring suck and you cannot hear him swallow.

6. Your baby is sluggish or slow to respond to stimulus, and does not sleep between feedings.

7. Your baby is not gaining weight or growing in length. Your doctor will direct you in the best strategy to correct this problem.

Any two consecutive days of deviation from what is listed above as normal should be reported immediately to your pediatrician.

Using the chart to keep track of your baby's vital health indicators can make the difference between healthy and unhealthy growth. If you wish, make copies of the chart and place it in a convenient location (on a refrigerator, above the crib, etc.). For your assurance record the results with a ($\sqrt{}$) mark for each occurrence of each healthy indicator. For example, six wet diapers on Monday should have six checks in the appropriate box. Knowing what to expect and measuring the expected results against the actual will provide you security and confidence as your baby grows.

HEALTHY BABY GROWTH CHART: Chart Two Weeks 2–4

— Summary of Each Day —

HEALTHY GROWTH INDICATORS	MON	TUE	WED	THU	FRI	SAT	SUN
Place a check (✔) for each feeding in a 24-hour period. (Minimum of 8.)							
Place a check (✔) for each wet diaper per day with clear urine. (Norm per day: 5 to 7.)							
Place a check (✔) for each wet diaper with yellow concentrated urine. (Norm per day: 0.)							
Place a check (✔) for each yellow stool. (For the first month, 2 to 5 or more, per day.)							

Any two consecutive days of deviation from what is listed as normal *should be reported immediately to your pediatrician.*

HEALTHY BABY GROWTH CHART: Chart Two Weeks 2–4

Summary of Each Day

HEALTHY GROWTH INDICATORS	MON	TUE	WED	THU	FRI	SAT	SUN
Place a check (✔) for each feeding in a 24-hour period. (Minimum of 8.)							
Place a check (✔) for each wet diaper per day with clear urine. (Norm per day: 5 to 7.)							
Place a check (✔) for each wet diaper with yellow concentrated urine. (Norm per day: 0.)							
Place a check (✔) for each yellow stool. (For the first month, 2 to 5 or more, per day.)							

Any two consecutive days of deviation from what is listed as normal *should be reported immediately to your pediatrician.*

© Gary Ezzo & Robert Bucknam

HEALTHY BABY GROWTH CHART: Chart Two Weeks 2–4

—— Summary of Each Day ——

HEALTHY GROWTH INDICATORS	MON	TUE	WED	THU	FRI	SAT	SUN
Place a check (✔) for each feeding in a 24-hour period. (Minimum of 8.)							
Place a check (✔) for each wet diaper per day with clear urine. (Norm per day: 5 to 7.)							
Place a check (✔) for each wet diaper with yellow concentrated urine. (Norm per day: 0.)							
Place a check (✔) for each yellow stool. (For the first month, 2 to 5 or more, per day.)							

Any two consecutive days of deviation from what is listed as normal *should be reported immediately to your pediatrician.*

© Gary Ezzo & Robert Bucknam

SIGNS OF ADEQUATE NUTRITION

Chart Three—Weeks Five through Ten

This third chart differs from the second only in the number of stools eliminated. Basically the rest of the chart is the same. Continue to monitor your baby's growth, especially after your baby starts sleeping through the night.

Here is the checklist for the next six weeks.

1. Your baby is nursing at least seven to eight times a day.

2. Your baby's stooling pattern again changes. Your baby may have several small stools or one large one. He may have several a day or one every couple of days.

3. Your baby should have six to eight wet diapers a day, some saturated.

4. Your baby's urine is clear, not yellow.

5. Your baby has a strong suck, you see milk, and you can hear an audible swallow.

6. You are seeing increasing signs of alertness during your baby's waketime.

7. Your baby is gaining weight and growing in length.

Unhealthy growth indicators are:

1. Your baby is not getting a minimum of seven feedings a day.

2. Your baby does not have the appropriate number of wet diapers given his age.

3. Your baby's urine is concentrated and bright yellow.

4. Your baby has a weak or tiring suck and you cannot hear him swallow.

5. Your baby is sluggish or slow to respond to stimulus, and does not sleep between feedings.

6. Your baby is not gaining weight or growing in length. Your doctor will direct you in the best strategy to correct this problem.

Any two consecutive days of deviation from what is listed above as normal should be reported immediately to your pediatrician.

Using the chart to keep track of your baby's vital health indicators can make the difference between healthy and unhealthy growth. If you wish, make copies of the chart and place it in a convenient location (on a refrigerator, above the crib, etc.). For your assurance, record the results with a (√) mark for each occurrence of each healthy indicator. For example, six wet diapers on Monday should have six checks in the appropriate box. Knowing what to expect and measuring the expected results against the actual will provide you security and confidence as your baby grows.

HEALTHY BABY GROWTH CHART: Chart Three Weeks 5–10

—— Summary of Each Day ——

HEALTHY GROWTH INDICATORS	MON	TUE	WED	THU	FRI	SAT	SUN
Place a check (✔) for each feeding. (Minimum should be 7-8 in a 24-hour period.)							
Place a check (✔) for each wet diaper per day with clear urine (Norm per day: 5 to 7.)							
Place a check (✔) for each wet diaper with yellow concentrated urine. (Norm per day: 0.)							
Place a check (✔) for each stool per day.							

Any two consecutive days of deviation from what is listed as normal *should be reported immediately to your pediatrician.*

© Gary Ezzo & Robert Bucknam

HEALTHY BABY GROWTH CHART: Chart Three Weeks 5–10

Summary of Each Day

HEALTHY GROWTH INDICATORS	MON.		TUE.		WED.		THU.		FRI.		SAT.		SUN.
Place a check (✔) for each feeding. (Minimum should be 7–8 in a 24-hour period.)													
Place a check (✔) for each wet diaper per day with clear urine (Norm per day: 5 to 7.)													
Place a check (✔) for each wet diaper with yellow concentrated urine. (Norm per day: 0.)													
Place a check (✔) for each stool per day.													

Any two consecutive days of deviation from what is listed as normal *should be reported immediately to your pediatrician.*

HEALTHY BABY GROWTH CHART: Chart Three Weeks 5–10

Summary of Each Day

HEALTHY GROWTH INDICATORS	MON.	TUE.	WED.	THU.	FRI.	SAT.	SUN.
Place a check (✔) for each feeding. (Minimum should be 7-8 in a 24-hour period.)							
Place a check (✔) for each wet diaper per day with clear urine (Norm per day: 5 to 7.)							
Place a check (✔) for each wet diaper with yellow concentrated urine. (Norm per day: 0.)							
Place a check (✔) for each stool per day.							

Any two consecutive days of deviation from what is listed as normal *should be reported immediately to your pediatrician.*

© Gary Ezzo & Robert Bucknam

HEALTHY BABY GROWTH CHART: Chart Three Weeks 5–10

— Summary of Each Day —

HEALTHY GROWTH INDICATORS	MON	TUE	WED	THU	FRI	SAT	SUN
Place a check (✔) for each feeding. (Minimum should be 7-8 in a 24-hour period.)							
Place a check (✔) for each wet diaper per day with clear urine (Norm per day: 5 to 7.)							
Place a check (✔) for each wet diaper with yellow concentrated urine. (Norm per day: 0.)							
Place a check (✔) for each stool per day.							

Any two consecutive days of deviation from what is listed as normal *should be reported immediately to your pediatrician.*

© Gary Ezzo & Robert Bucknam

HEALTHY BABY GROWTH CHART: Chart Three Weeks 5–10

Summary of Each Day

HEALTHY GROWTH INDICATORS	MON.	TUE.	WED.	THU.	FRI.	SAT.	SUN.
Place a check (✔) for each feeding. (Minimum should be 7-8 in a 24-hour period.)							
Place a check (✔) for each wet diaper per day with clear urine (Norm per day: 5 to 7.)							
Place a check (✔) for each wet diaper with yellow concentrated urine. (Norm per day: 0.)							
Place a check (✔) for each stool per day.							

Any two consecutive days of deviation from what is listed as normal *should be reported immediately to your pediatrician.*

© Gary Ezzo & Robert Bucknam

HEALTHY BABY GROWTH CHART: Chart Three Weeks 5–10

Summary of Each Day

HEALTHY GROWTH INDICATORS	MON	TUE	WED	THU	FRI	SAT	SUN
Place a check (✔) for each feeding. (Minimum should be 7-8 in a 24-hour period.)							
Place a check (✔) for each wet diaper per day with clear urine (Norm per day: 5 to 7.)							
Place a check (✔) for each wet diaper with yellow concentrated urine. (Norm per day: 0.)							
Place a check (✔) for each stool per day.							

Any two consecutive days of deviation from what is listed as normal *should be reported immediately to your pediatrician.*